IT'S A
BOY

To: _____

From: _____

IT'S A
BOY

A BABY BLUES® BOOK

by Rick Kirkman and Jerry Scott

**Andrews McMeel
Publishing, LLC**

Kansas City • Sydney • London

Baby Blues® is syndicated internationally by King Features Syndicate, Inc. For information, write King Features Syndicate, Inc., 300 West Fifty-Seventh Street, New York, New York 10019.

10 11 12 13 14 WKT 10 9 8 7 6 5 4 3 2 1

ISBN-13: 978-0-7407-9166-6
ISBN-10: 0-7407-9166-4

Library of Congress Control Number: 2009936124

www.andrewsmcmeel.com

Find *Baby Blues*® on the Web at
www.babyblues.com.

ATTENTION: SCHOOLS AND BUSINESSES
Andrews McMeel books are available at quantity discounts with bulk purchase for educational, business, or sales promotional use. For information, please write to: Special Sales Department, Andrews McMeel Publishing, LLC, 1130 Walnut Street, Kansas City, Missouri 64106.

CHAPTER 1
PREGNANCY

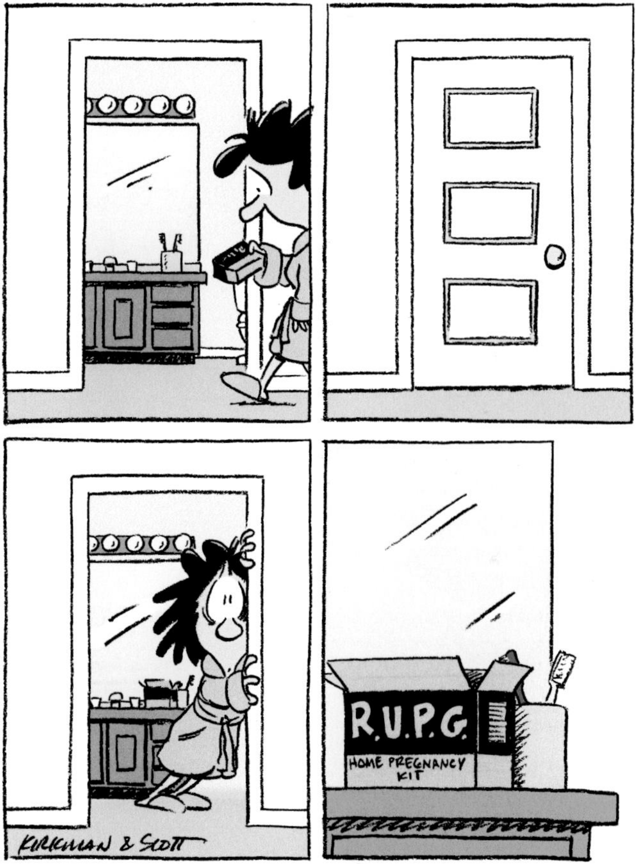
R.U.P.G.
HOME PREGNANCY KIT
KIRKMAN & SCOTT

I CAN'T BELIEVE I'M PREGNANT ALREADY!
WE WANT TO HAVE ANOTHER BABY, BUT I NEVER THOUGHT IT WOULD HAPPEN SO FAST!

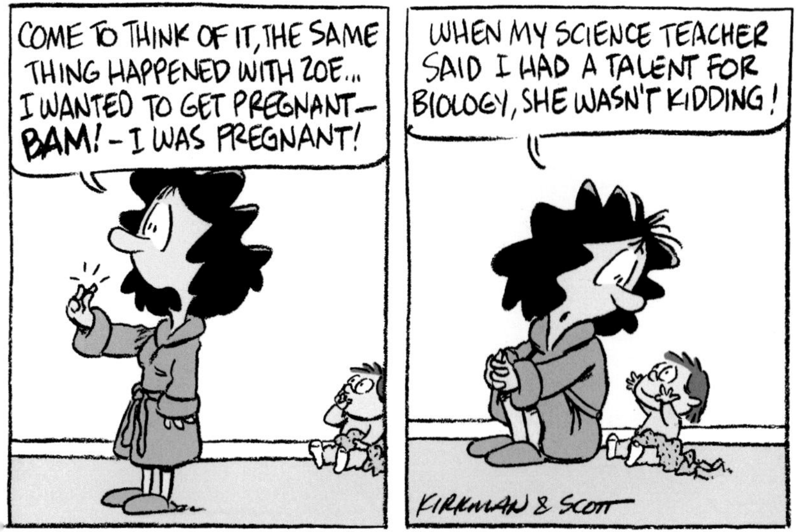
COME TO THINK OF IT, THE SAME THING HAPPENED WITH ZOE... I WANTED TO GET PREGNANT— BAM! —I WAS PREGNANT!
WHEN MY SCIENCE TEACHER SAID I HAD A TALENT FOR BIOLOGY, SHE WASN'T KIDDING!
KIRKMAN & SCOTT

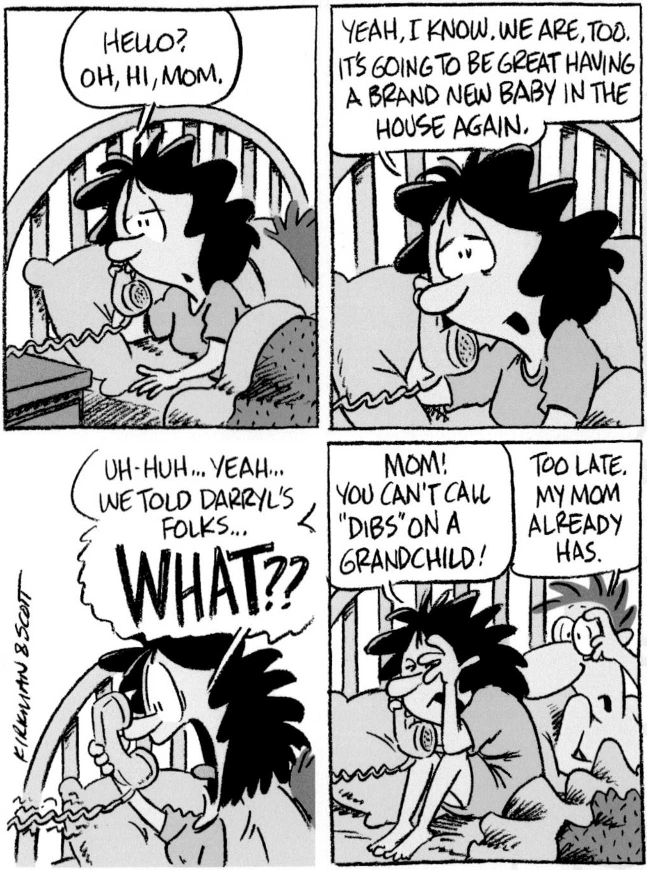
HELLO? OH, HI, MOM.
YEAH, I KNOW. WE ARE, TOO. IT'S GOING TO BE GREAT HAVING A BRAND NEW BABY IN THE HOUSE AGAIN.
UH-HUH... YEAH... WE TOLD DARRYL'S FOLKS...
WHAT??
MOM! YOU CAN'T CALL "DIBS" ON A GRANDCHILD!
TOO LATE. MY MOM ALREADY HAS.
KIRKMAN & SCOTT

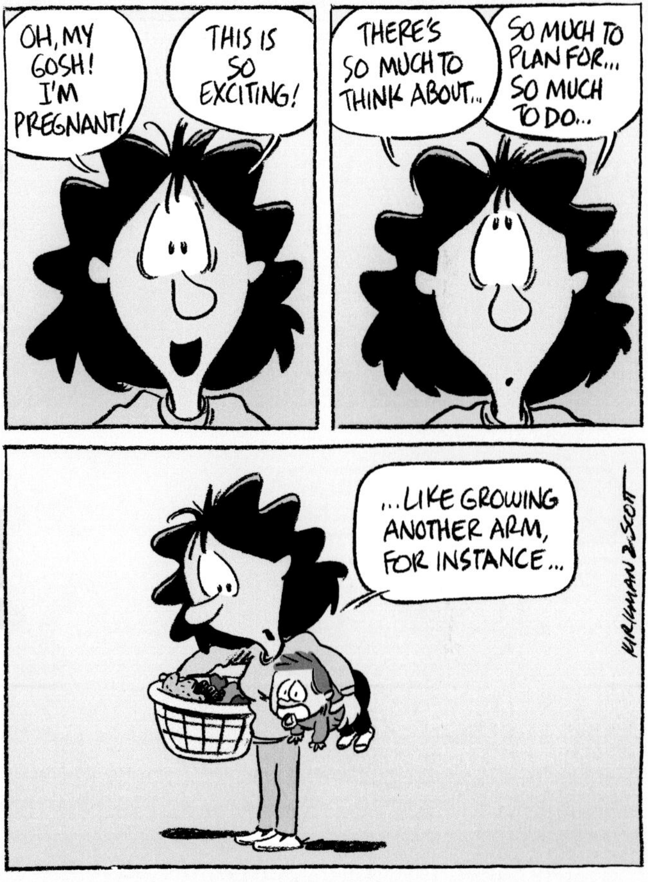
OH, MY GOSH! I'M PREGNANT!
THIS IS SO EXCITING!
THERE'S SO MUCH TO THINK ABOUT...
SO MUCH TO PLAN FOR... SO MUCH TO DO...
...LIKE GROWING ANOTHER ARM, FOR INSTANCE...
KIRKMAN & SCOTT

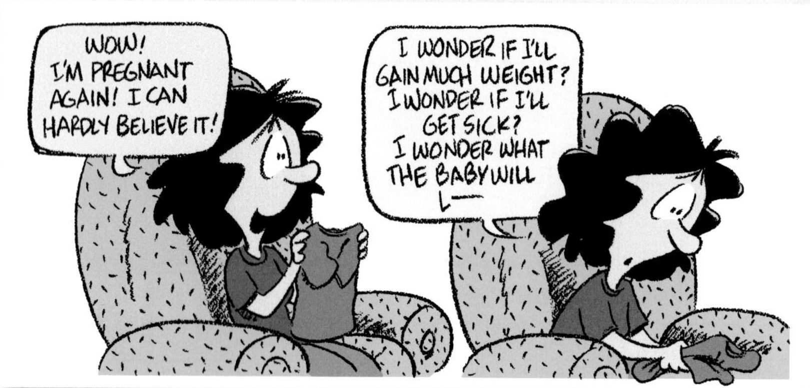
WOW! I'M PREGNANT AGAIN! I CAN HARDLY BELIEVE IT!
I WONDER IF I'LL GAIN MUCH WEIGHT? I WONDER IF I'LL GET SICK? I WONDER WHAT THE BABY WILL L—

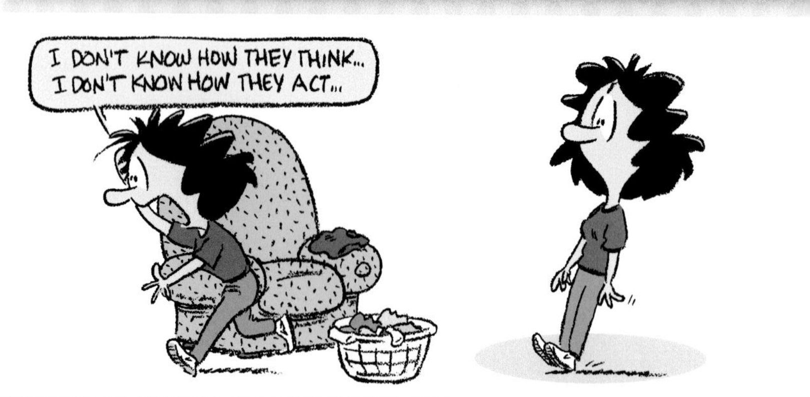
I DON'T KNOW HOW THEY THINK... I DON'T KNOW HOW THEY ACT...

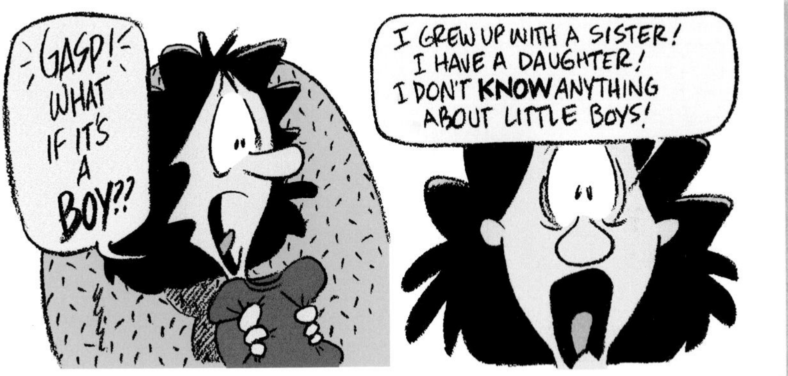
GASP! WHAT IF IT'S A BOY??
I GREW UP WITH A SISTER! I HAVE A DAUGHTER! I DON'T KNOW ANYTHING ABOUT LITTLE BOYS!

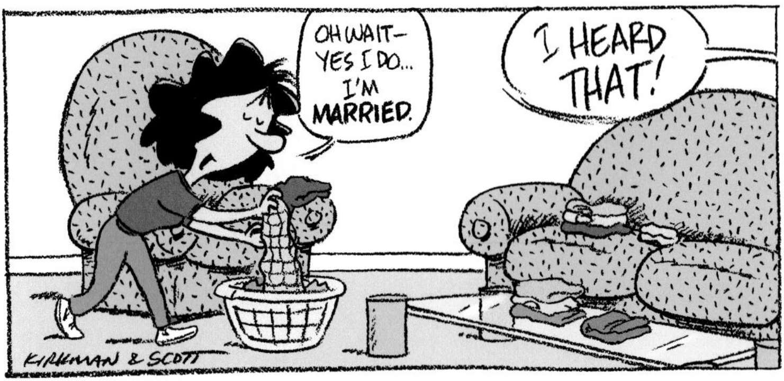
OH WAIT- YES I DO... I'M MARRIED.
I HEARD THAT!
KIRKMAN & SCOTT

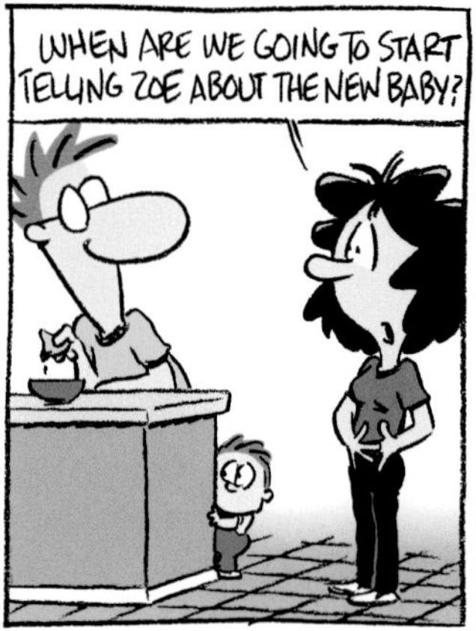
WHEN ARE WE GOING TO START TELLING ZOE ABOUT THE NEW BABY?

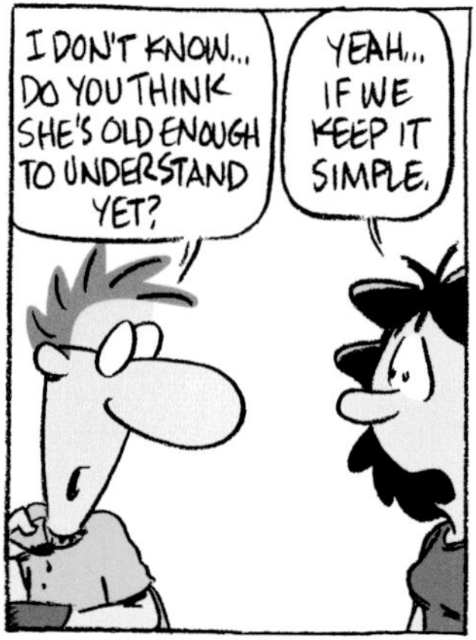
I DON'T KNOW... DO YOU THINK SHE'S OLD ENOUGH TO UNDERSTAND YET?
YEAH... IF WE KEEP IT SIMPLE.

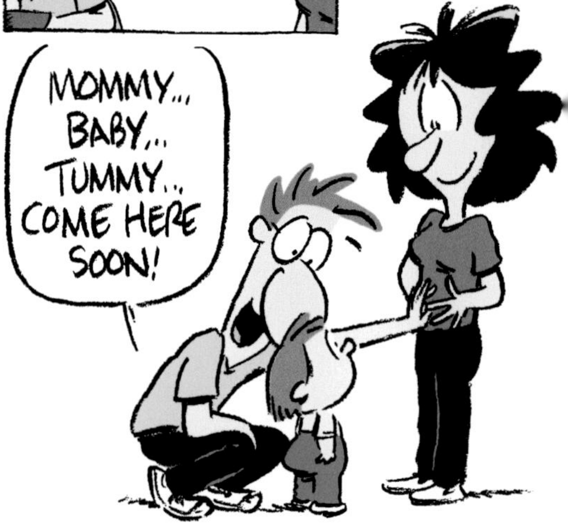
MOMMY... BABY... TUMMY... COME HERE SOON!

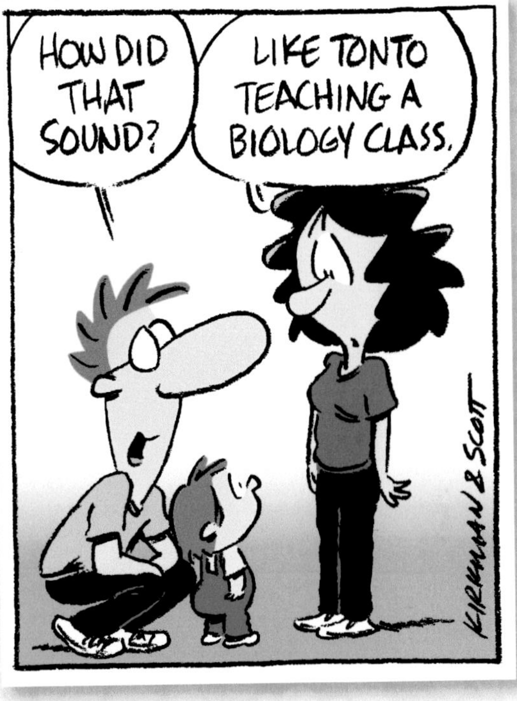
HOW DID THAT SOUND?
LIKE TONTO TEACHING A BIOLOGY CLASS.
KIRKMAN & SCOTT

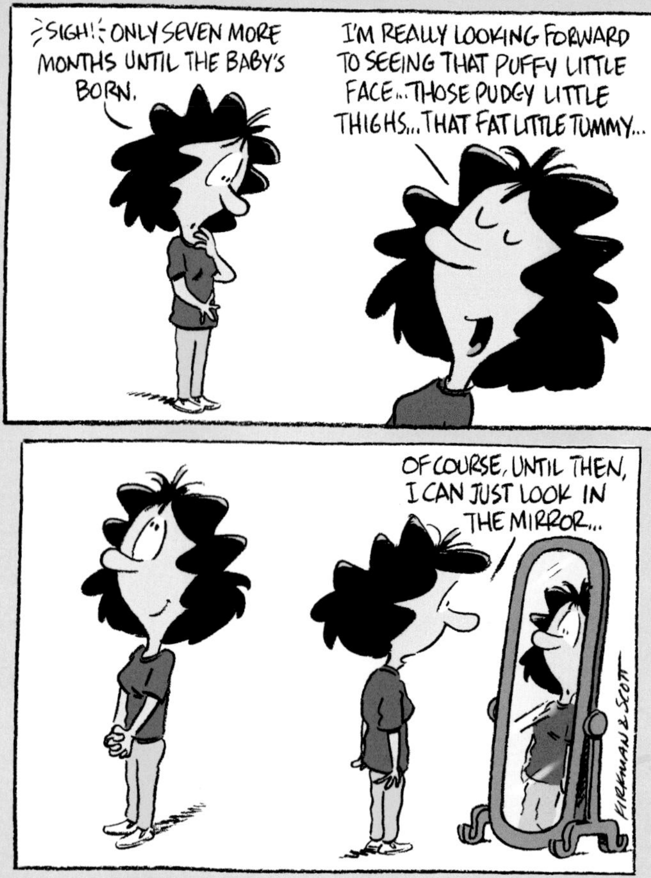
SIGH! ONLY SEVEN MORE MONTHS UNTIL THE BABY'S BORN.
I'M REALLY LOOKING FORWARD TO SEEING THAT PUFFY LITTLE FACE...THOSE PUDGY LITTLE THIGHS...THAT FAT LITTLE TUMMY...
OF COURSE, UNTIL THEN, I CAN JUST LOOK IN THE MIRROR...
KIRKMAN & SCOTT

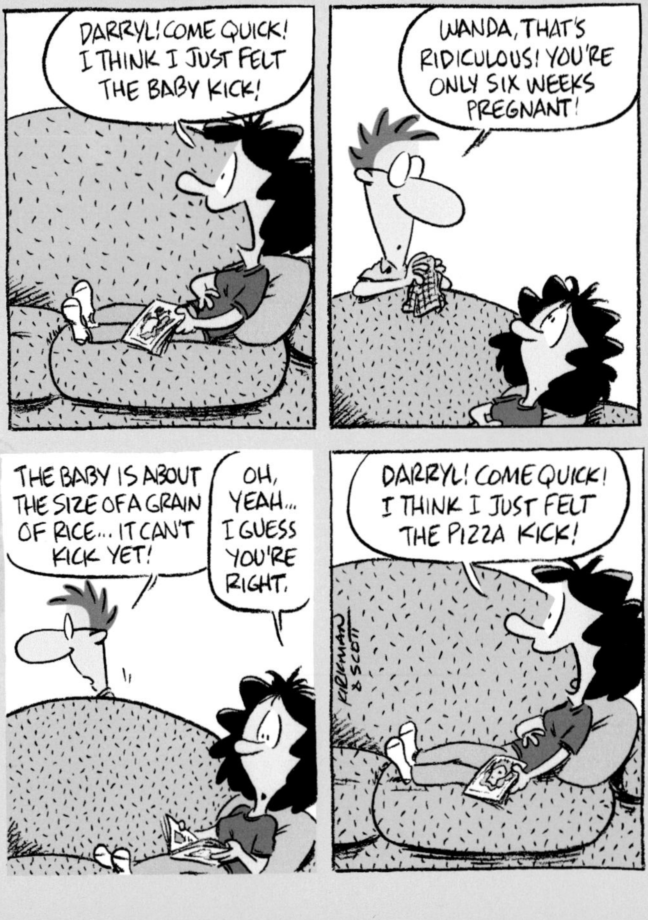
DARRYL! COME QUICK! I THINK I JUST FELT THE BABY KICK!
WANDA, THAT'S RIDICULOUS! YOU'RE ONLY SIX WEEKS PREGNANT!
THE BABY IS ABOUT THE SIZE OF A GRAIN OF RICE... IT CAN'T KICK YET!
OH, YEAH... I GUESS YOU'RE RIGHT.
DARRYL! COME QUICK! I THINK I JUST FELT THE PIZZA KICK!
KIRKMAN & SCOTT

WELL, IF YOU DON'T HAVE ANY OTHER QUESTIONS, I GUESS WE'LL SEE YOU NEXT MONTH.
THANKS, DR. WEST.
NANCY WILL GIVE YOU SOME BASIC LITERATURE ON MAIN-TAINING A HEALTHY PREGNANCY.
KIRKMAN & SCOTT

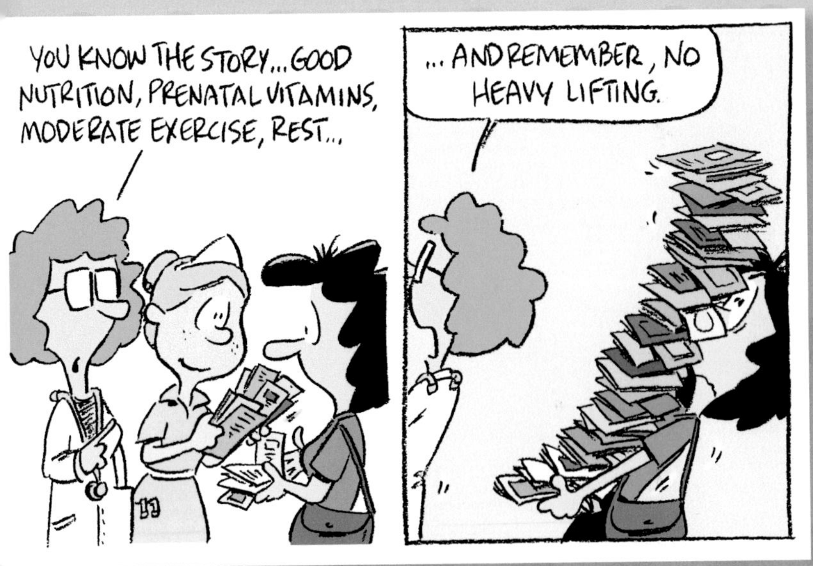
YOU KNOW THE STORY... GOOD NUTRITION, PRENATAL VITAMINS, MODERATE EXERCISE, REST...
... AND REMEMBER, NO HEAVY LIFTING.

OH, DARRYL! THERE'S OUR BABY!
YOU KNOW WHAT, HONEY? IT LOOKS LIKE YOU!
REALLY?
SURE! LOOK AT THE PROFILE! LOOK AT THAT BEAUTIFUL LITTLE HEAD!
KIRKMAN & SCOTT

THAT'S NOT THE HEAD.
IN THAT CASE, IT LOOKS LIKE ME.

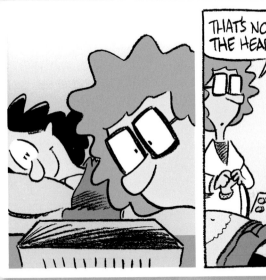

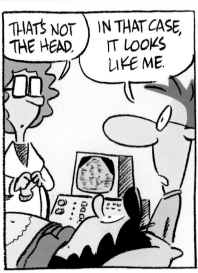

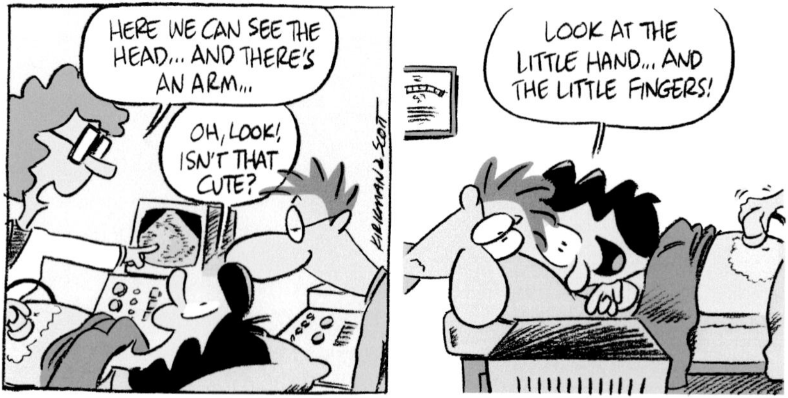
HERE WE CAN SEE THE HEAD... AND THERE'S AN ARM...
OH, LOOK! ISN'T THAT CUTE?
KIRKMAN & SCOTT
LOOK AT THE LITTLE HAND... AND THE LITTLE FINGERS!

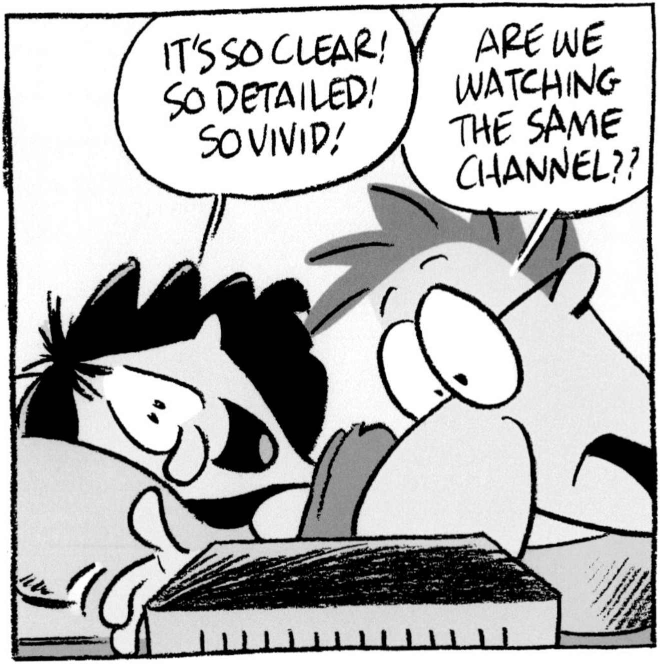
IT'S SO CLEAR! SO DETAILED! SO VIVID!
ARE WE WATCHING THE SAME CHANNEL??

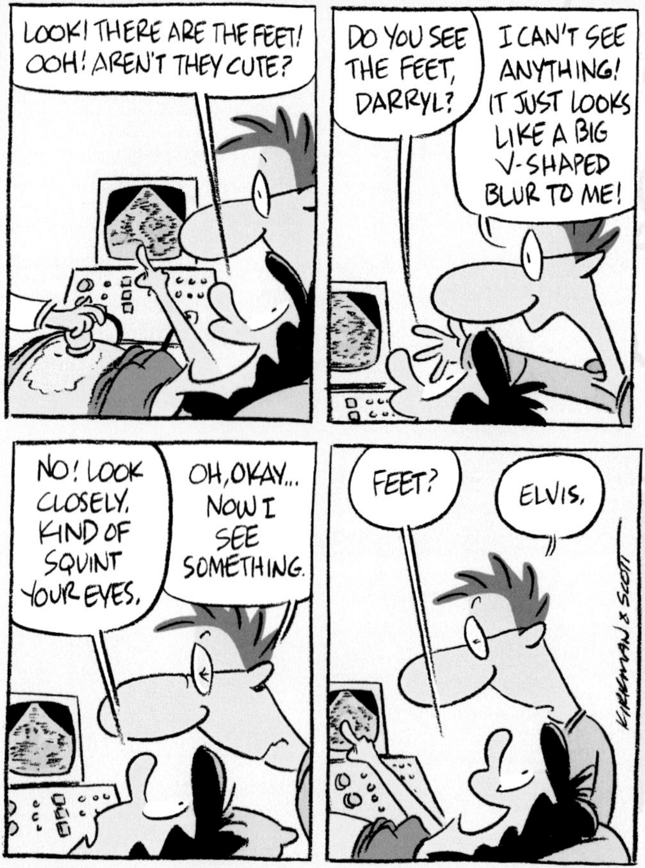

LOOK! THERE ARE THE FEET! OOH! AREN'T THEY CUTE?
DO YOU SEE THE FEET, DARRYL?
I CAN'T SEE ANYTHING! IT JUST LOOKS LIKE A BIG V-SHAPED BLUR TO ME!
NO! LOOK CLOSELY. KIND OF SQUINT YOUR EYES.
OH, OKAY... NOW I SEE SOMETHING.
FEET?
ELVIS.
KIRKMAN & SCOTT

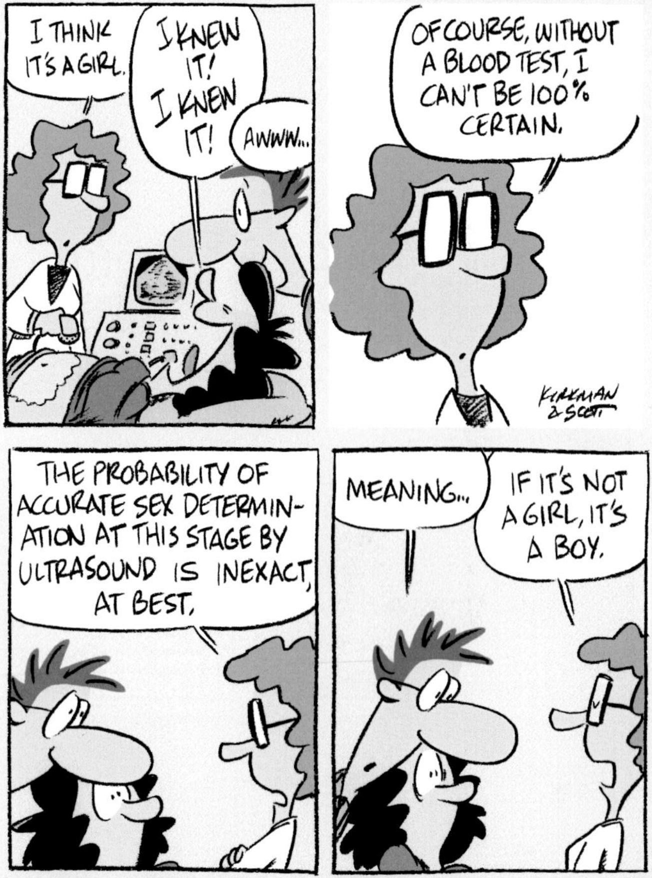
I THINK IT'S A GIRL.
I KNEW IT! I KNEW IT!
AWWW...
OF COURSE, WITHOUT A BLOOD TEST, I CAN'T BE 100% CERTAIN.
KIRKMAN & SCOTT
THE PROBABILITY OF ACCURATE SEX DETERMIN-ATION AT THIS STAGE BY ULTRASOUND IS INEXACT, AT BEST.
MEANING...
IF IT'S NOT A GIRL, IT'S A BOY.

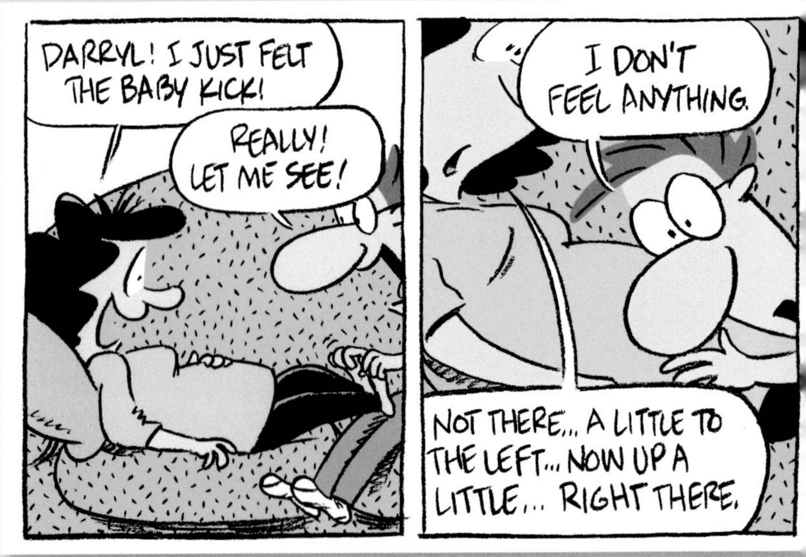
DARRYL! I JUST FELT THE BABY KICK!
REALLY! LET ME SEE!
I DON'T FEEL ANYTHING.
NOT THERE... A LITTLE TO THE LEFT... NOW UP A LITTLE... RIGHT THERE.

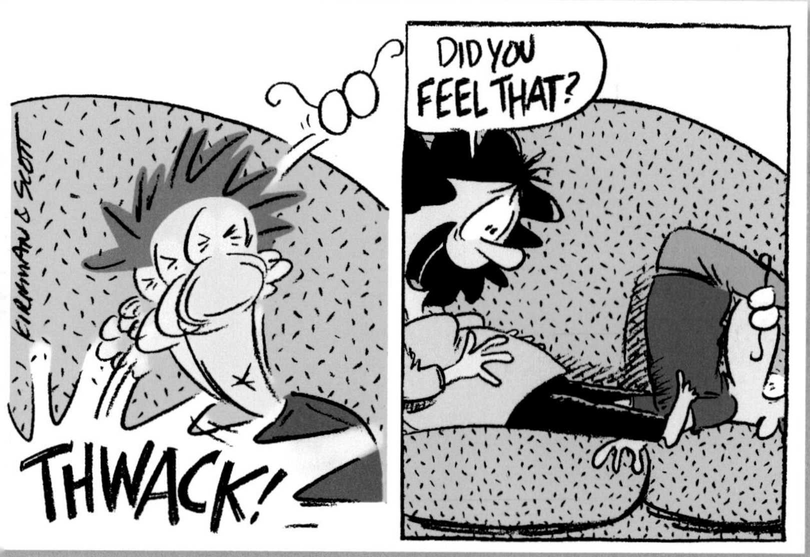
KIRKMAN & SCOTT
THWACK!
DID YOU FEEL THAT?

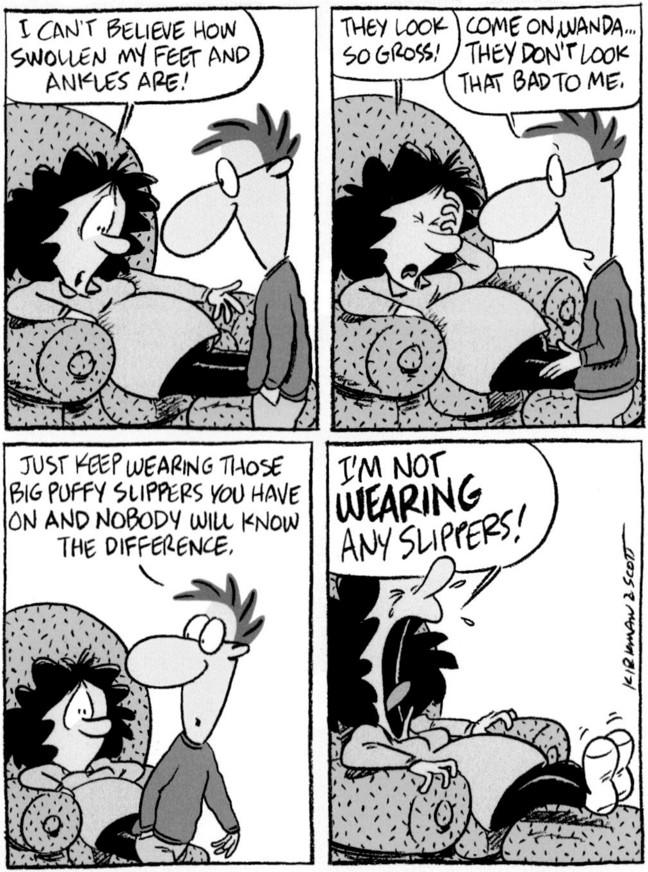
I CAN'T BELIEVE HOW SWOLLEN MY FEET AND ANKLES ARE!
THEY LOOK SO GROSS!
COME ON, WANDA... THEY DON'T LOOK THAT BAD TO ME.
JUST KEEP WEARING THOSE BIG PUFFY SLIPPERS YOU HAVE ON AND NOBODY WILL KNOW THE DIFFERENCE.
I'M NOT WEARING ANY SLIPPERS!
KIRKMAN & SCOTT

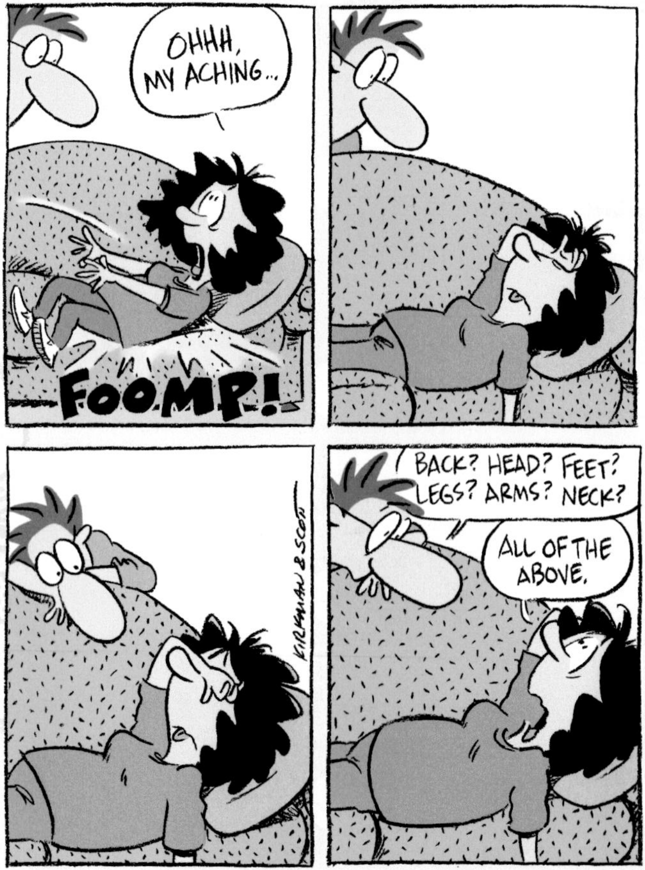
OHHH, MY ACHING...
FOOMP!
KIRKMAN & SCOTT
BACK? HEAD? FEET? LEGS? ARMS? NECK?
ALL OF THE ABOVE.

CHAPTER 2

BIRTH

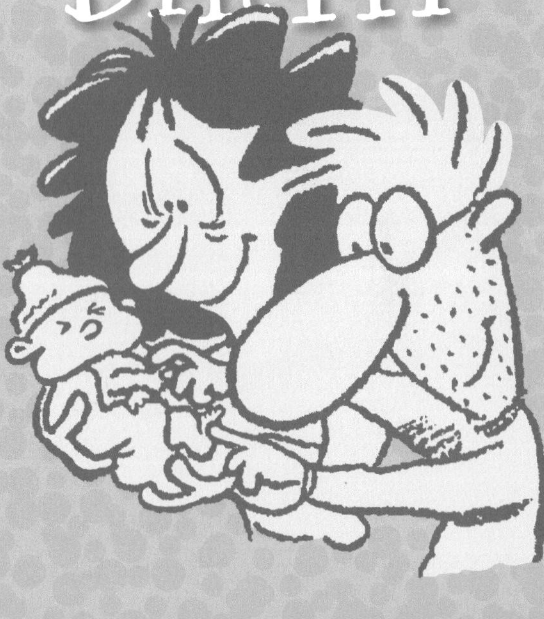

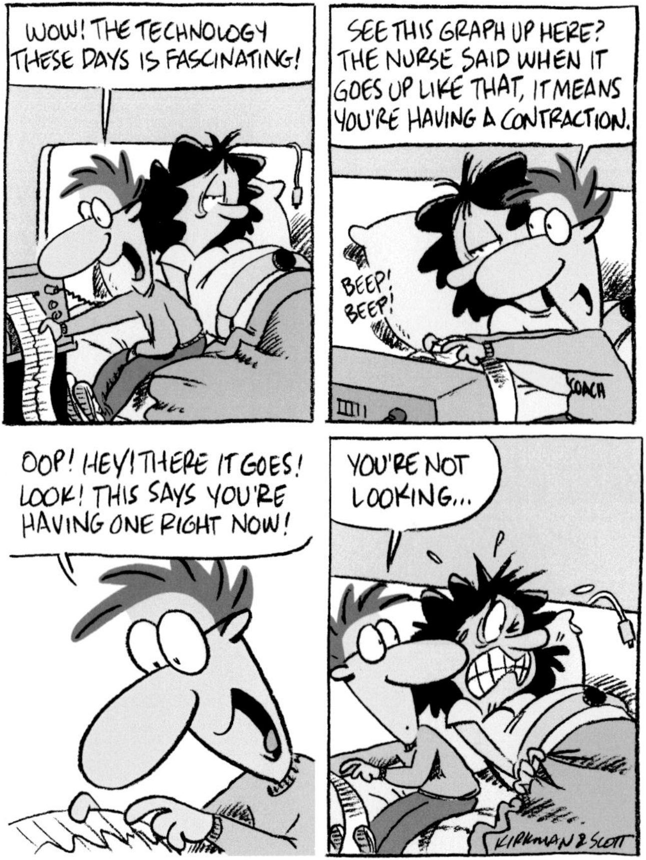
WOW! THE TECHNOLOGY THESE DAYS IS FASCINATING!
SEE THIS GRAPH UP HERE? THE NURSE SAID WHEN IT GOES UP LIKE THAT, IT MEANS YOU'RE HAVING A CONTRACTION.
BEEP! BEEP!
COACH
OOP! HEY! THERE IT GOES! LOOK! THIS SAYS YOU'RE HAVING ONE RIGHT NOW!
YOU'RE NOT LOOKING...
KIRKMAN & SCOTT

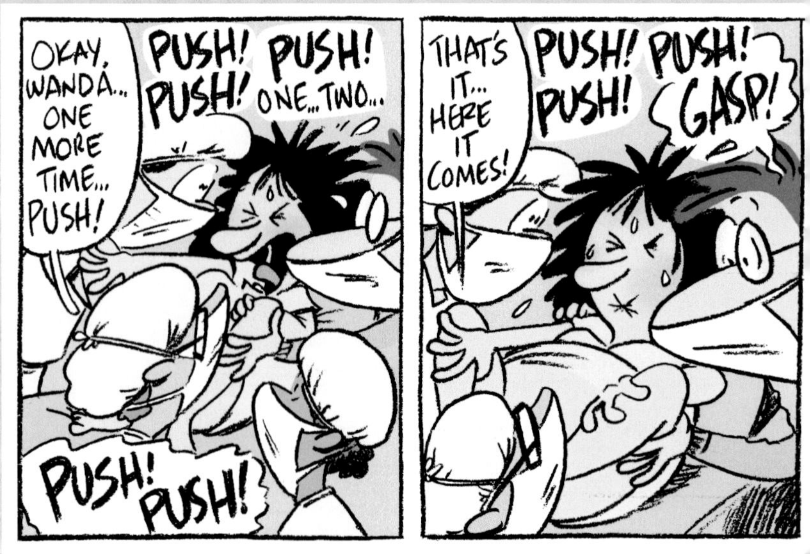
OKAY, WANDA... ONE MORE TIME... PUSH!
PUSH! PUSH!
PUSH! ONE... TWO...
PUSH! PUSH!
THAT'S IT... HERE IT COMES!
PUSH! PUSH!
PUSH! GASP!

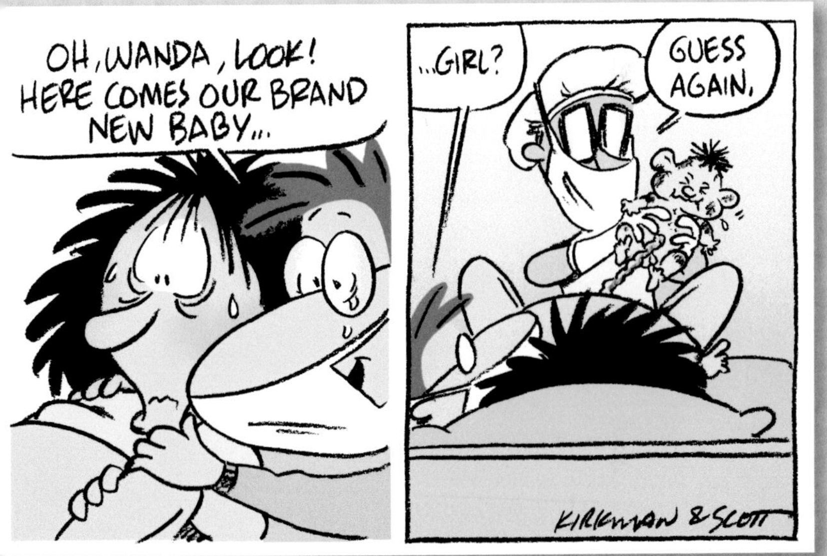
OH, WANDA, LOOK! HERE COMES OUR BRAND NEW BABY...
...GIRL?
GUESS AGAIN.
KIRKMAN & SCOTT

HERE COMES THE SON

SUNG TO THE TUNE OF THE BEATLES' "HERE COMES THE SUN"

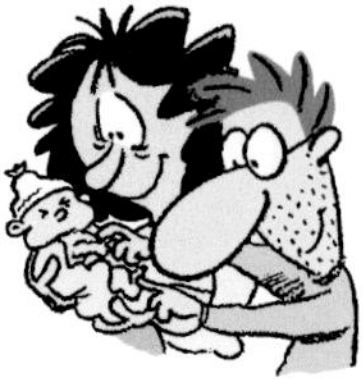

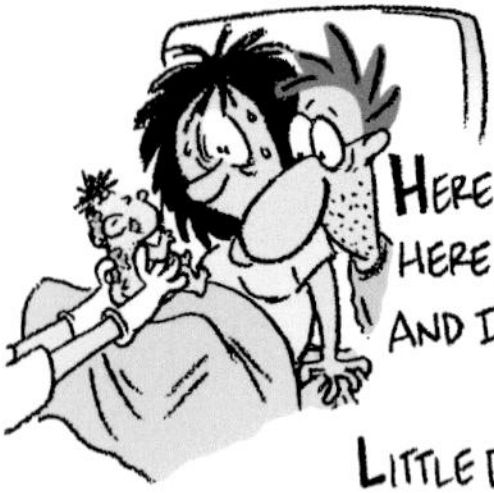

HERE COMES A SON (doo 'n doo-doo)
HERE COMES A SON,
AND I SAY, "IT'S A FRIGHT!"

LITTLE DARLIN', IT WAS A
SHOCK TO SEE YOUR GENDER!
LITTLE DARLIN', WE THOUGHT
A GIRL WAS TO APPEAR!

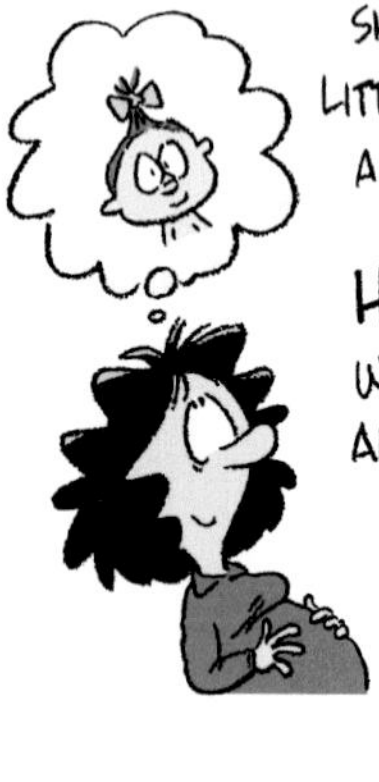

HERE COMES A SON (doo 'n doo-doo)
WE'RE BOTH SO STUNNED,
AND I SAY, "YOU'RE A SIGHT!"

KIRKMAN & SCOTT

LITTLE DARLIN', THE BLOOD'S
RETURNING TO OUR FACES.
LITTLE DARLIN', WE SEE THE YEARS
THAT YOU'LL BE HERE.

HE IS OUR SON.
LOOK WHAT WE'VE DONE.
AND I SAY, "HE'S JUST RIGHT."

SON, SON, SON, HERE WE COME!
SON, SON, SON-OF-A-GUN!
SON, SON, SON, HERE WE COME!
SON, SON, SON-OF-A-GUN!
SON, SON, SON, HERE WE COME!

LITTLE DARLIN', YOUR VERY FIRST SUNRISE IS DAWNING.
LITTLE DARLIN', IT'S JUST AN HOUR SINCE YOU GOT HERE.

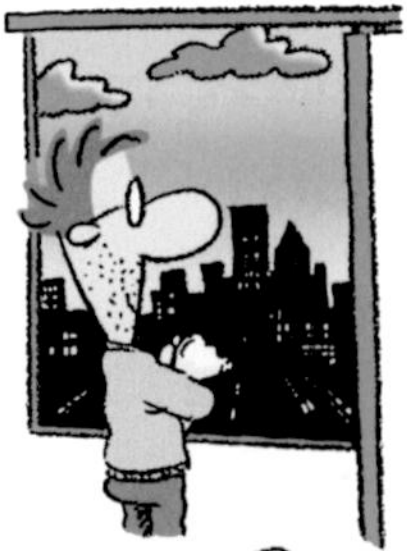

HERE COMES THE SUN (doo 'n doo-doo)
WE HAVE A SON,
AND I SAY, "IT'S SO RIGHT!"

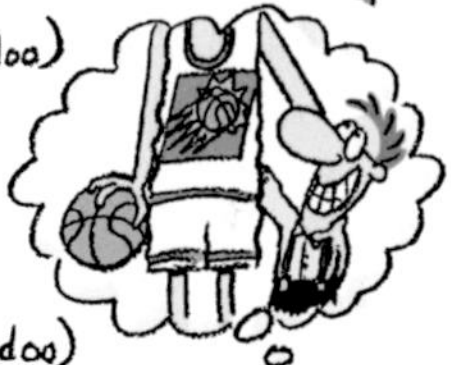

HERE COMES THE SUN (doo 'n doo-doo)
WE HAVE A SON.
IT'S SO RIGHT!
IT'S SO RIGHT!

(WITH APOLOGIES TO GEORGE HARRISON)

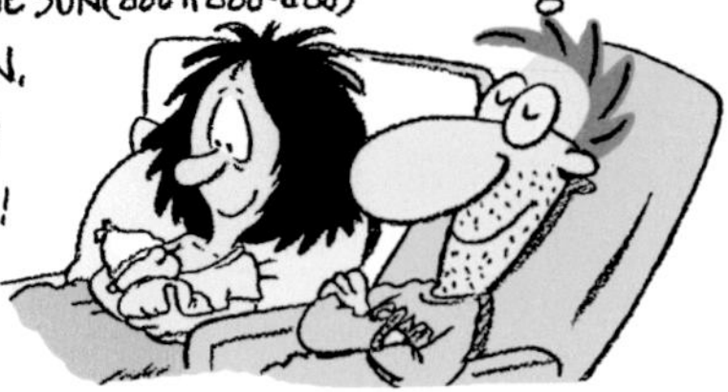

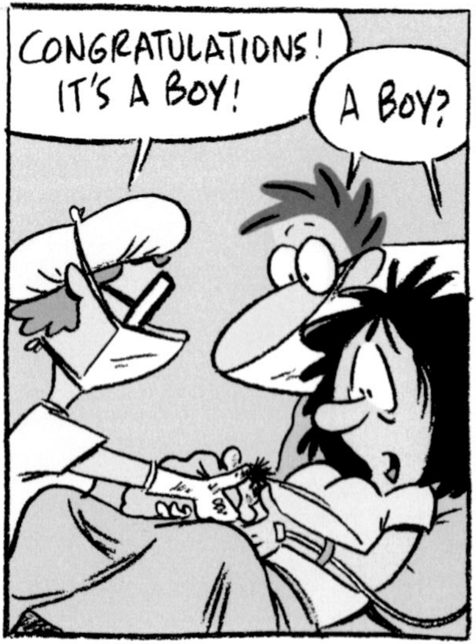
CONGRATULATIONS! IT'S A BOY!
A BOY?

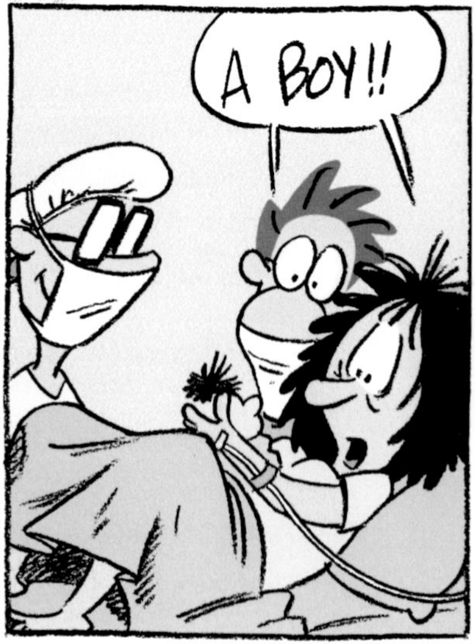
A BOY!!

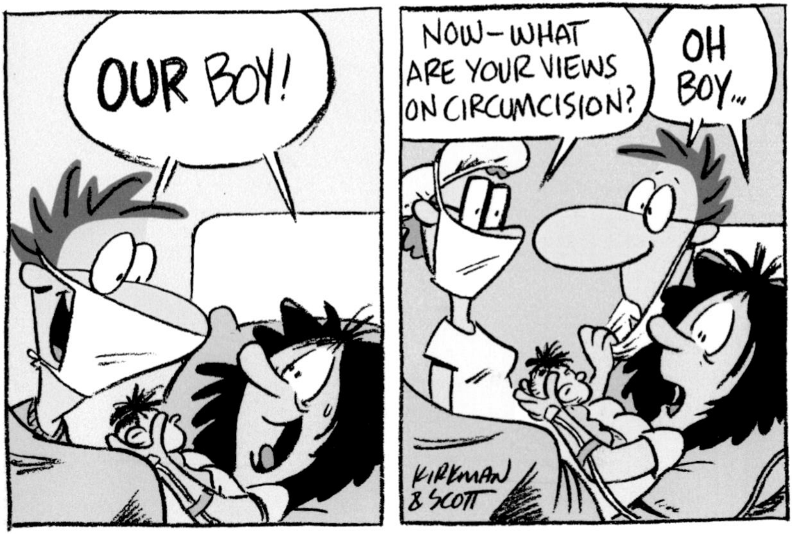
OUR BOY!
NOW—WHAT ARE YOUR VIEWS ON CIRCUMCISION?
OH BOY...
KIRKMAN & SCOTT

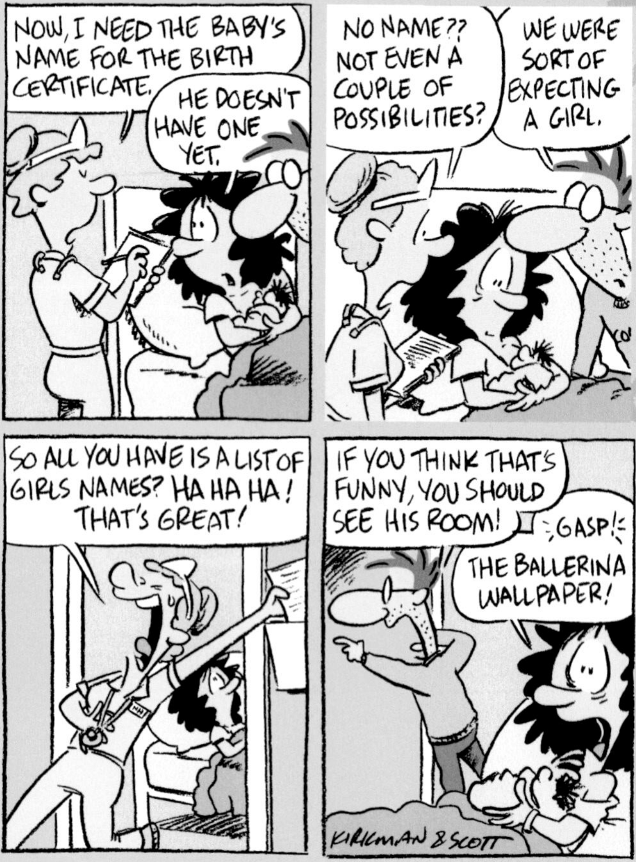
NOW, I NEED THE BABY'S NAME FOR THE BIRTH CERTIFICATE.
HE DOESN'T HAVE ONE YET.
NO NAME?? NOT EVEN A COUPLE OF POSSIBILITIES?
WE WERE SORT OF EXPECTING A GIRL.
SO ALL YOU HAVE IS A LIST OF GIRLS NAMES? HA HA HA! THAT'S GREAT!
IF YOU THINK THAT'S FUNNY, YOU SHOULD SEE HIS ROOM!
GASP!
THE BALLERINA WALLPAPER!
KIRKMAN & SCOTT

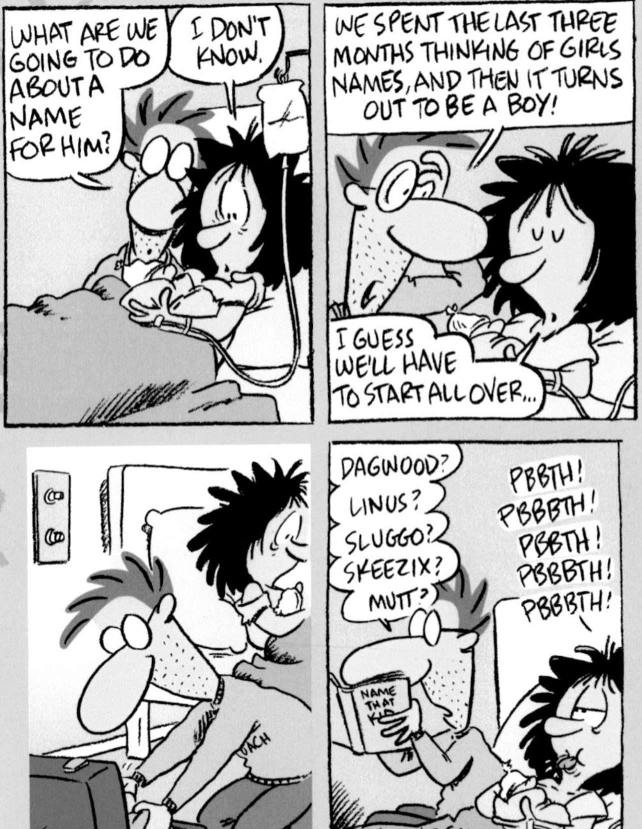
WHAT ARE WE GOING TO DO ABOUT A NAME FOR HIM?
I DON'T KNOW.
WE SPENT THE LAST THREE MONTHS THINKING OF GIRLS NAMES, AND THEN IT TURNS OUT TO BE A BOY!
I GUESS WE'LL HAVE TO START ALL OVER...
DAGWOOD?
LINUS?
SLUGGO?
SKEEZIX?
MUTT?
PBBTH!
PBBBTH!
PBBTH!
PBBBTH!
PBBBTH!
NAME THAT
KIRKMAN & SCOTT

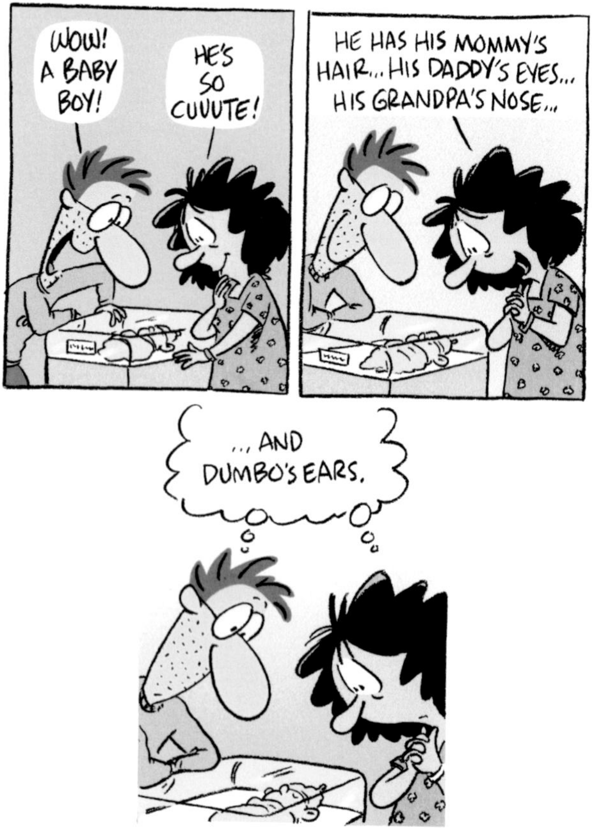
WOW! A BABY BOY!
HE'S SO CUUUTE!
HE HAS HIS MOMMY'S HAIR... HIS DADDY'S EYES... HIS GRANDPA'S NOSE...
... AND DUMBO'S EARS.

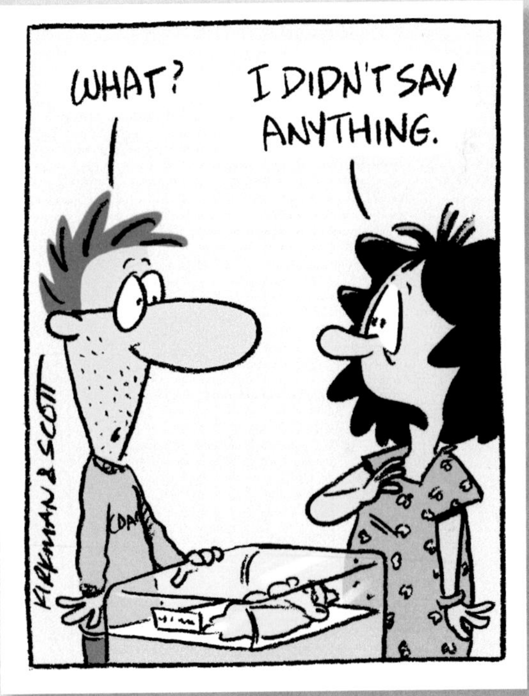
WHAT?
I DIDN'T SAY ANYTHING.
KIRKMAN & SCOTT

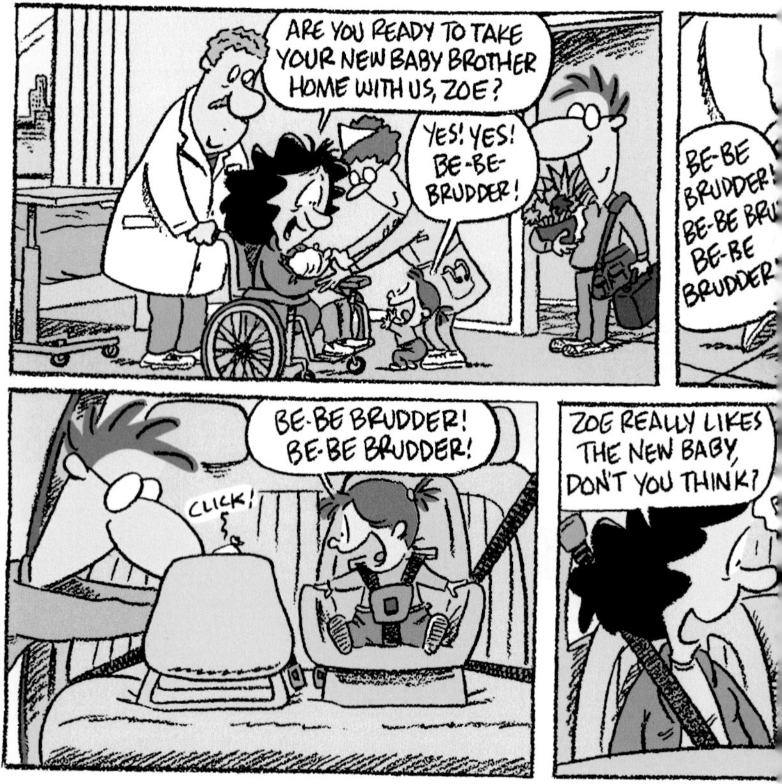
ARE YOU READY TO TAKE YOUR NEW BABY BROTHER HOME WITH US, ZOE?
YES! YES! BE-BE-BRUDDER!
BE-BE BRUDDER!
BE-BE BRUDDER! BE-BE BRUDDER!
CLICK!
ZOE REALLY LIKES THE NEW BABY, DON'T YOU THINK?

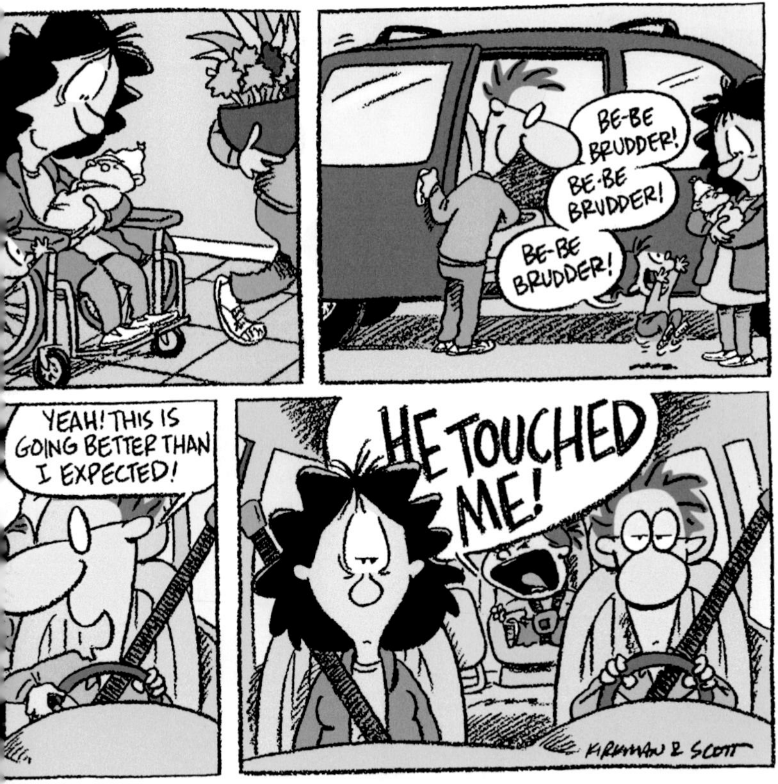
BE-BE BRUDDER!
BE-BE BRUDDER!
BE-BE BRUDDER!
YEAH! THIS IS GOING BETTER THAN I EXPECTED!
HE TOUCHED ME!
KIRKMAN & SCOTT

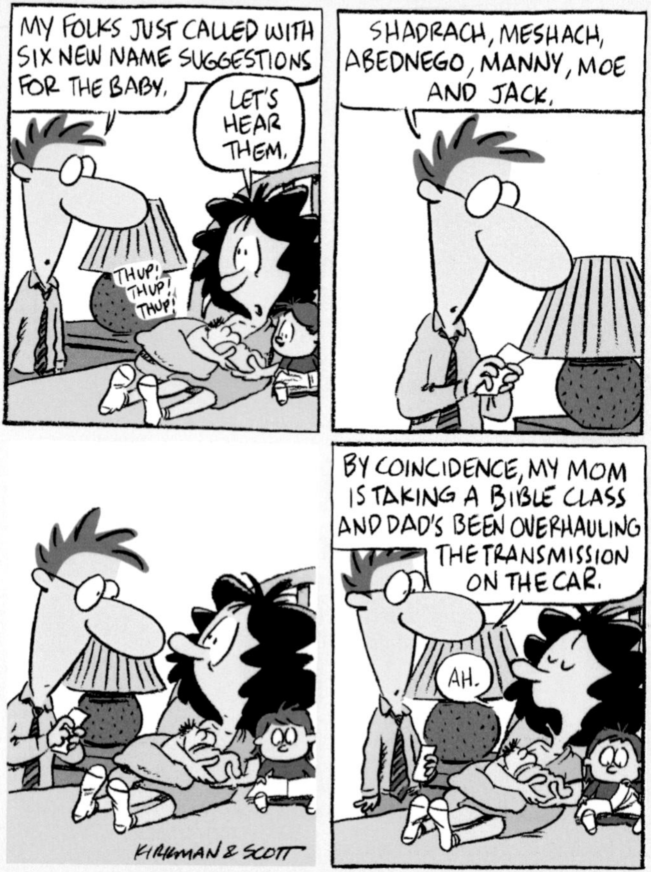
MY FOLKS JUST CALLED WITH SIX NEW NAME SUGGESTIONS FOR THE BABY.
LET'S HEAR THEM.
THUP! THUP! THUP!
SHADRACH, MESHACH, ABEDNEGO, MANNY, MOE AND JACK.
BY COINCIDENCE, MY MOM IS TAKING A BIBLE CLASS AND DAD'S BEEN OVERHAULING THE TRANSMISSION ON THE CAR.
AH.
KIRKMAN & SCOTT

DO YOU LIKE YOUR NEW BABY BROTHER, ZOE?
YES... WHATZ IZ NAME?
WELL, HE DOESN'T REALLY HAVE ONE YET...
WHAT DO YOU THINK WE SHOULD NAME HIM?
KIRKMAN & SCOTT
BIG BIRD!
NO... I DON'T THINK "BIG BIRD" IS GOING TO WORK.
WHY NOT? I LIKE IT BETTER THAN ANYTHING YOUR PARENTS HAVE SUGGESTED.
WAAAAAAAAAAA!

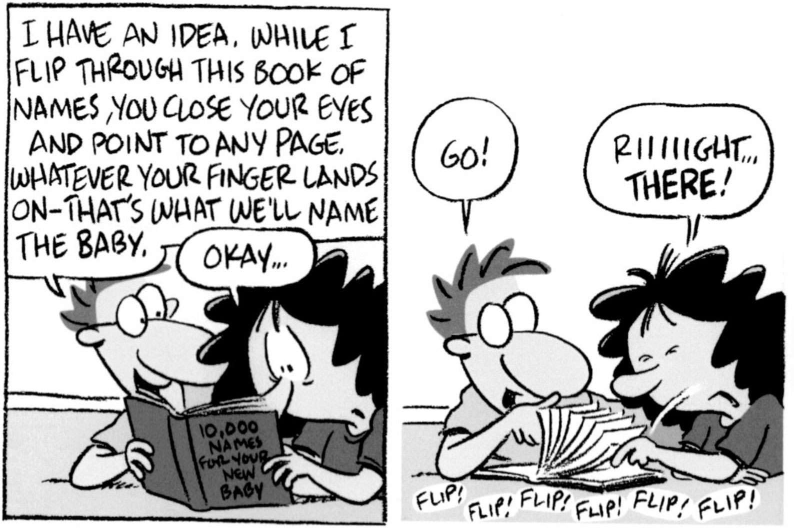
I HAVE AN IDEA. WHILE I FLIP THROUGH THIS BOOK OF NAMES, YOU CLOSE YOUR EYES AND POINT TO ANY PAGE. WHATEVER YOUR FINGER LANDS ON–THAT'S WHAT WE'LL NAME THE BABY.
OKAY...
10,000 NAMES FOR YOUR NEW BABY
GO!
RIIIIIGHT... THERE!
FLIP! FLIP! FLIP! FLIP! FLIP! FLIP!

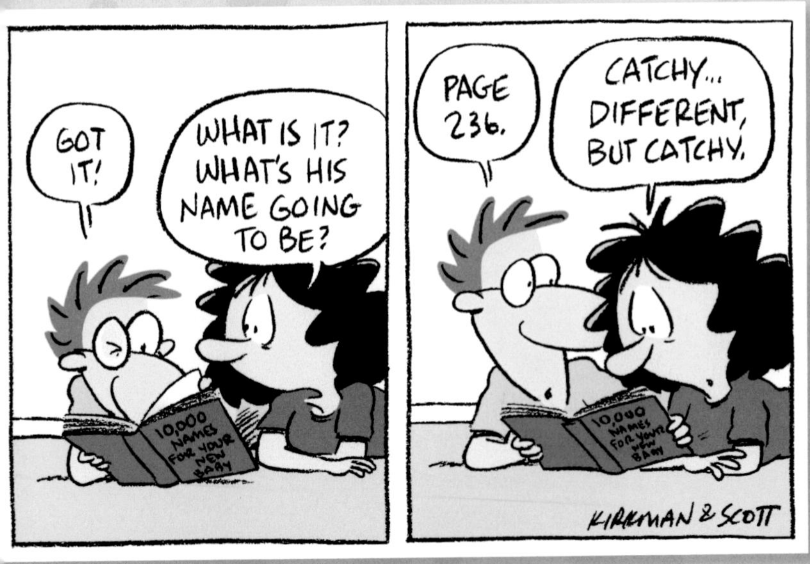
GOT IT!
WHAT IS IT? WHAT'S HIS NAME GOING TO BE?
10,000 NAMES FOR YOUR NEW BABY
PAGE 236.
CATCHY... DIFFERENT, BUT CATCHY.
10,000 NAMES FOR YOUR NEW BABY
KIRKMAN & SCOTT

CHAPTER 3

SIBLINGS

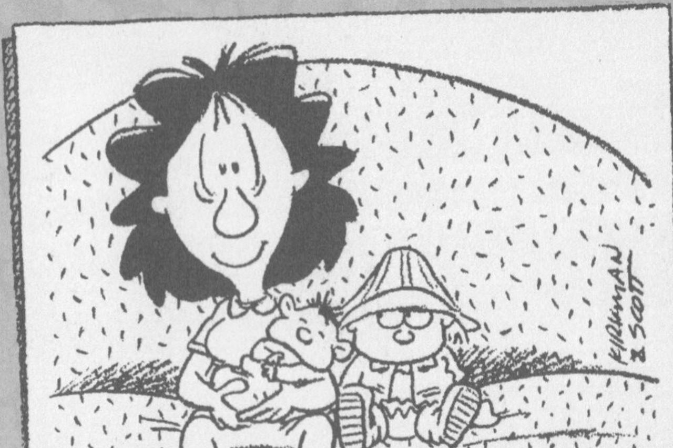
KIRKMAN & SCOTT

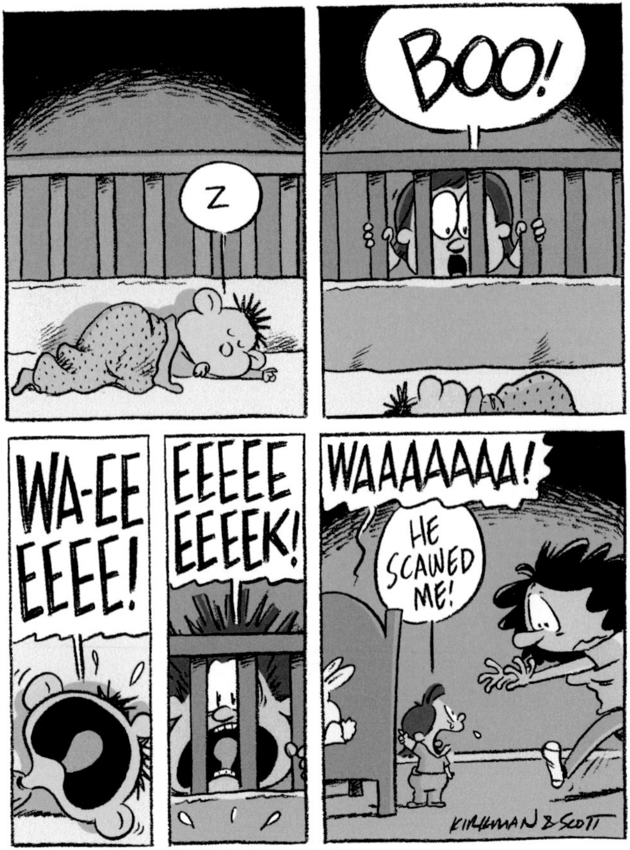
Z
BOO!
WA-EE EEEE!
EEEEE EEEEK!
WAAAAAAA!
HE SCAWED ME!
KIRKMAN & SCOTT

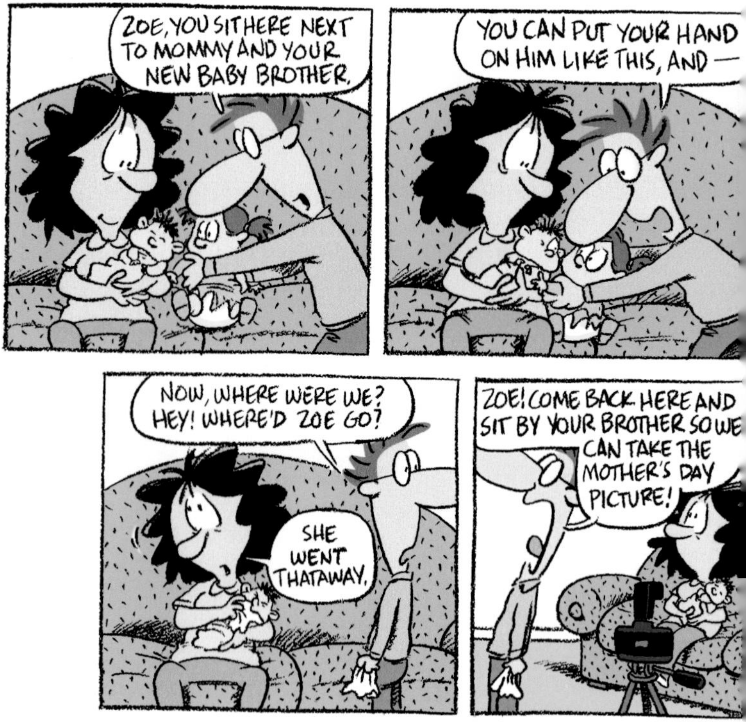
ZOE, YOU SIT HERE NEXT TO MOMMY AND YOUR NEW BABY BROTHER.
YOU CAN PUT YOUR HAND ON HIM LIKE THIS, AND —
NOW, WHERE WERE WE? HEY! WHERE'D ZOE GO?
SHE WENT THATAWAY.
ZOE! COME BACK HERE AND SIT BY YOUR BROTHER SO WE CAN TAKE THE MOTHER'S DAY PICTURE!

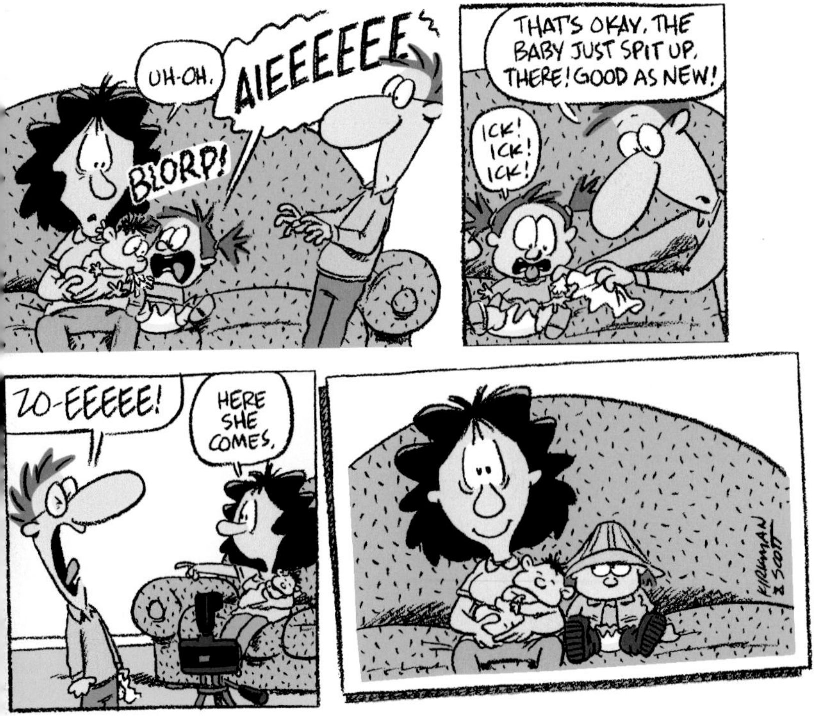
UH-OH.
AIEEEEEEE
BLORP!
THAT'S OKAY. THE BABY JUST SPIT UP. THERE! GOOD AS NEW!
ICK! ICK! ICK!
ZO-EEEEE!
HERE SHE COMES.
KIRKMAN & SCOTT

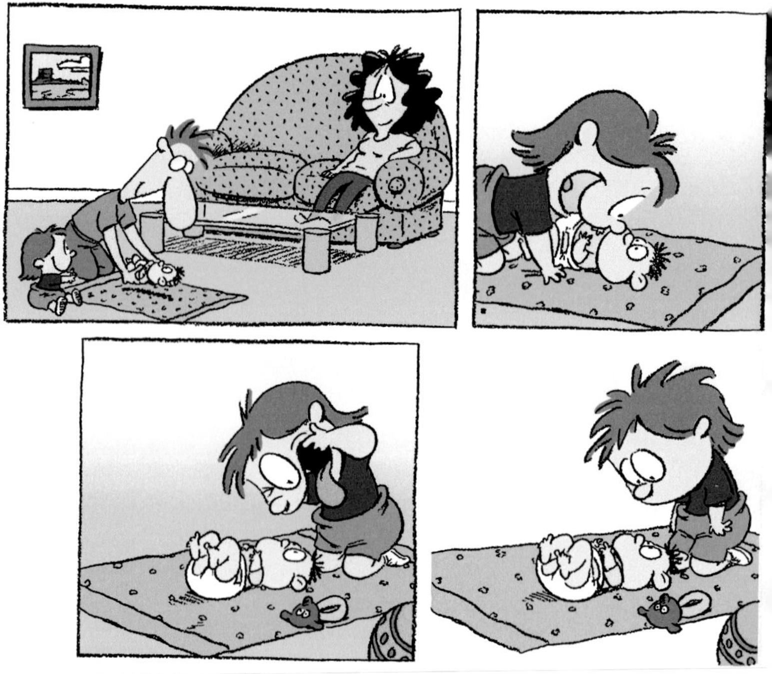

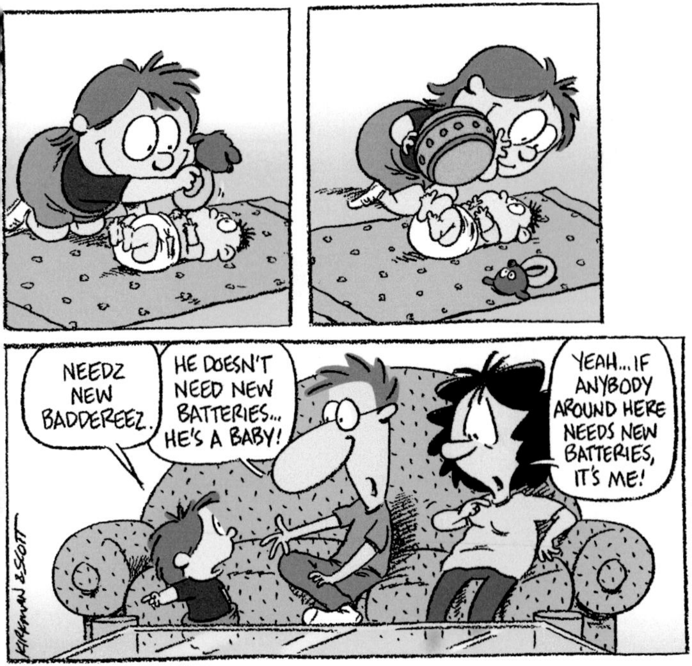
NEEDZ NEW BADDEREEZ.
HE DOESN'T NEED NEW BATTERIES... HE'S A BABY!
YEAH... IF ANYBODY AROUND HERE NEEDS NEW BATTERIES, IT'S ME!
KIRKMAN & SCOTT

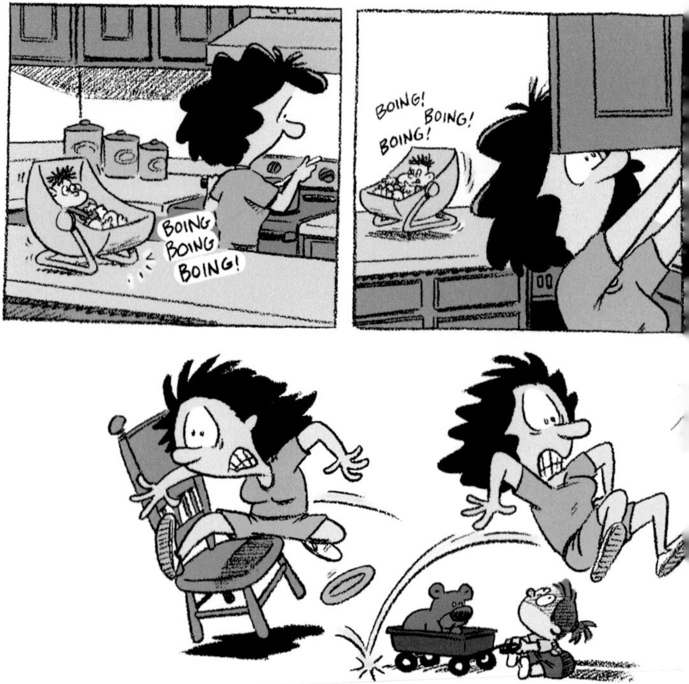
BOING
BOING
BOING!
BOING!
BOING!
BOING!

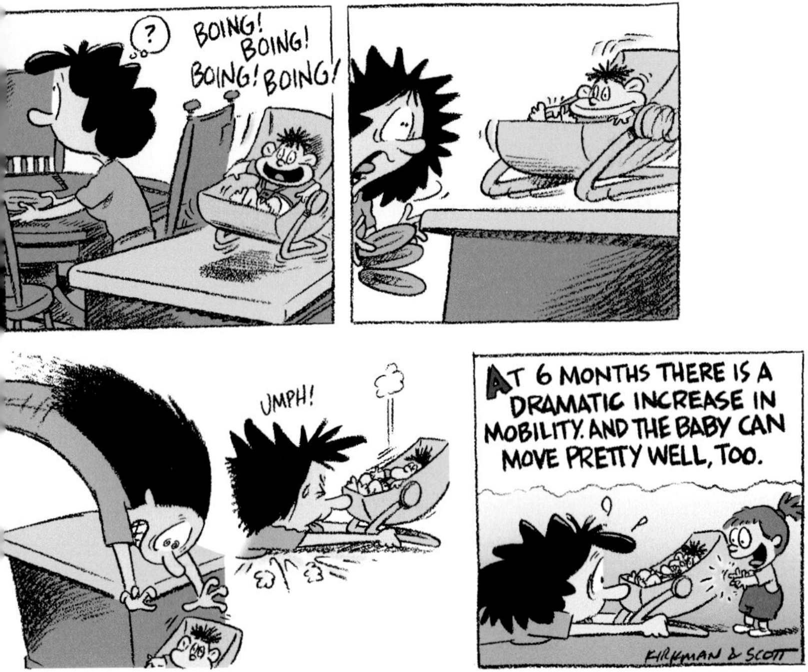
?
BOING! BOING! BOING! BOING!
UMPH!
AT 6 MONTHS THERE IS A DRAMATIC INCREASE IN MOBILITY. AND THE BABY CAN MOVE PRETTY WELL, TOO.
KIRKMAN & SCOTT

OW! OWIE! OWIE! HAMMIE IS PUWWING MY HAIR!
LET GO, HAMMIE! THAT'S NOT NICE!
IS HAMMIE IN TWOUBLE?
NO, YOU ONLY GET IN TROUBLE FOR DOING SOMETHING OVER AND OVER AFTER YOU'VE BEEN TOLD NOT TO DO IT.

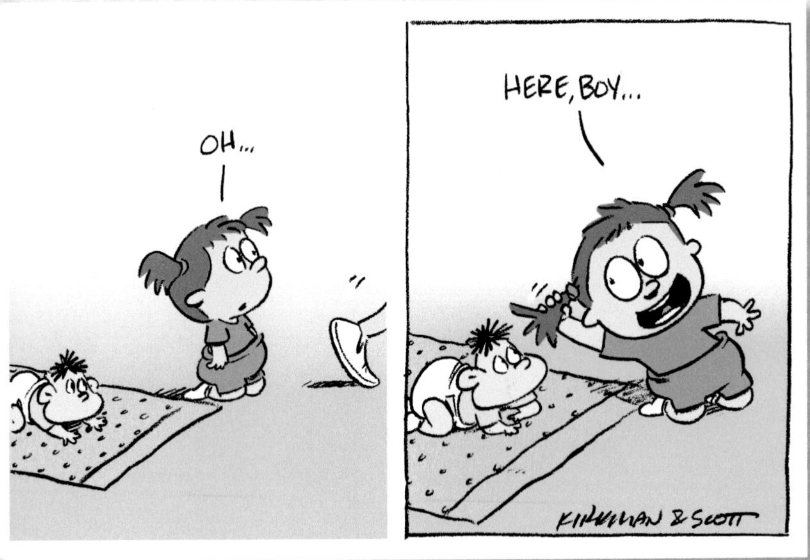
OH...
HERE, BOY...
KIRKMAN & SCOTT

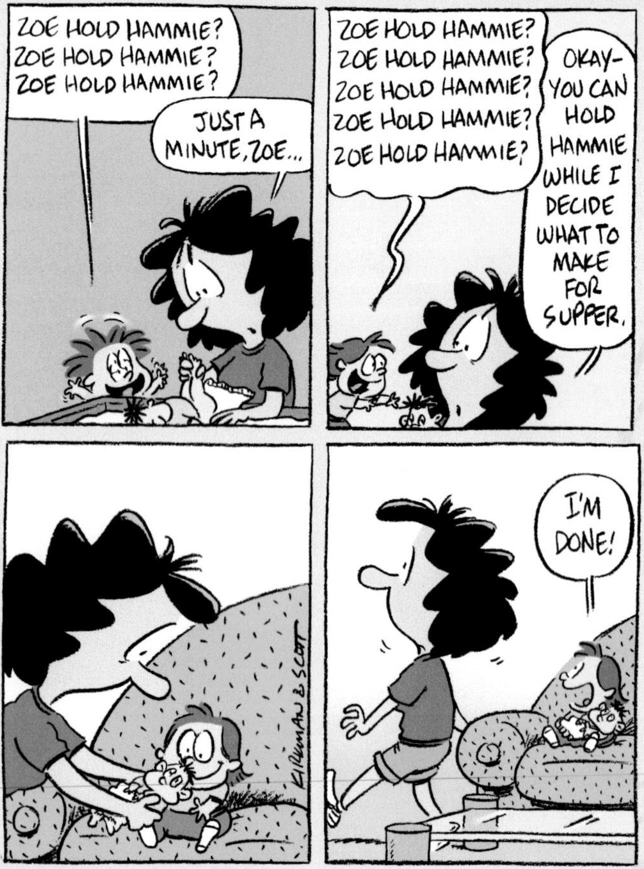
ZOE HOLD HAMMIE?
ZOE HOLD HAMMIE?
ZOE HOLD HAMMIE?
JUST A MINUTE, ZOE...
ZOE HOLD HAMMIE?
ZOE HOLD HAMMIE?
ZOE HOLD HAMMIE?
ZOE HOLD HAMMIE?
ZOE HOLD HAMMIE?
OKAY- YOU CAN HOLD HAMMIE WHILE I DECIDE WHAT TO MAKE FOR SUPPER.
KIRKMAN & SCOTT
I'M DONE!

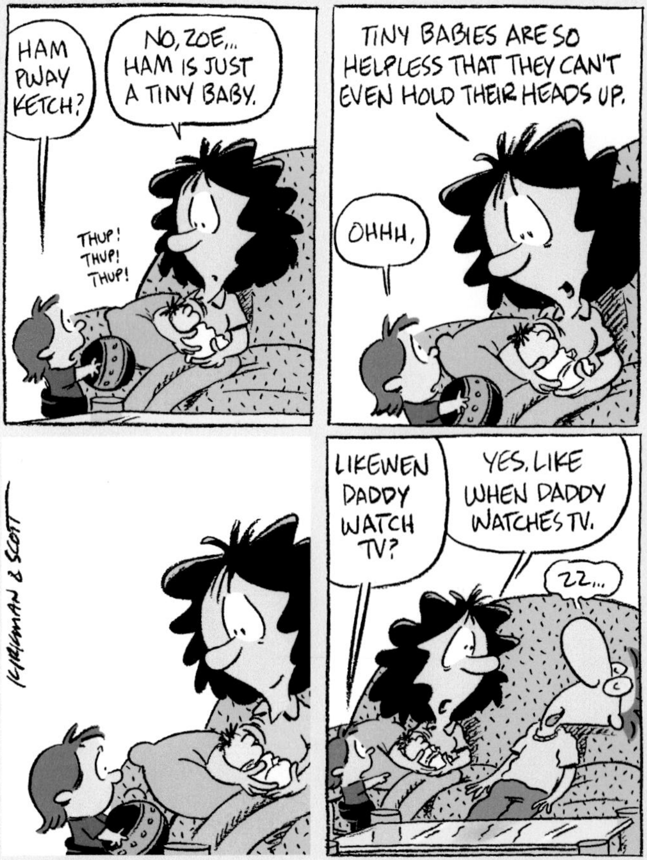
HAM PWAY KETCH?
NO, ZOE,... HAM IS JUST A TINY BABY.
THUP! THUP! THUP!
TINY BABIES ARE SO HELPLESS THAT THEY CAN'T EVEN HOLD THEIR HEADS UP.
OHHH,
KIRKMAN & SCOTT
LIKEWEN DADDY WATCH TV?
YES, LIKE WHEN DADDY WATCHES TV.
ZZ...

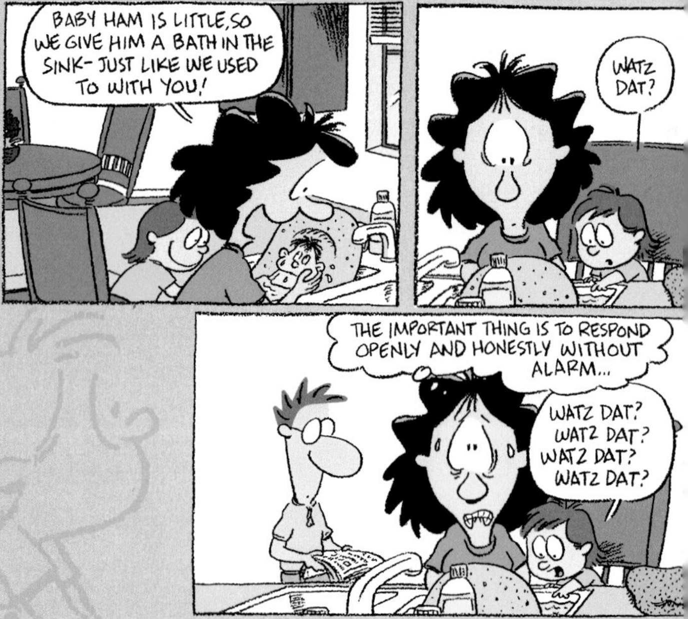
BABY HAM IS LITTLE, SO WE GIVE HIM A BATH IN THE SINK- JUST LIKE WE USED TO WITH YOU!
WATZ DAT?
THE IMPORTANT THING IS TO RESPOND OPENLY AND HONESTLY WITHOUT ALARM...
WATZ DAT? WATZ DAT? WATZ DAT? WATZ DAT?

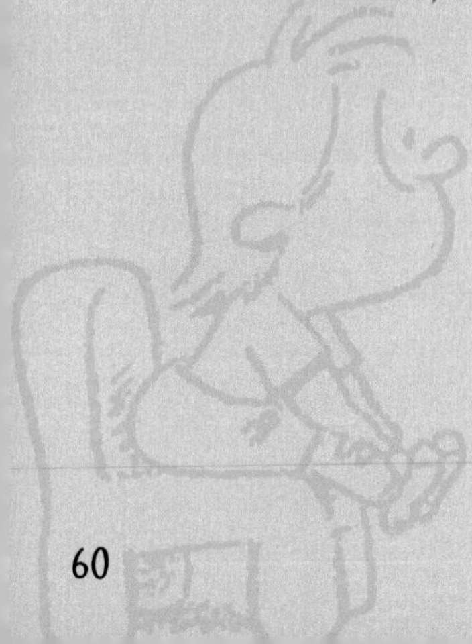

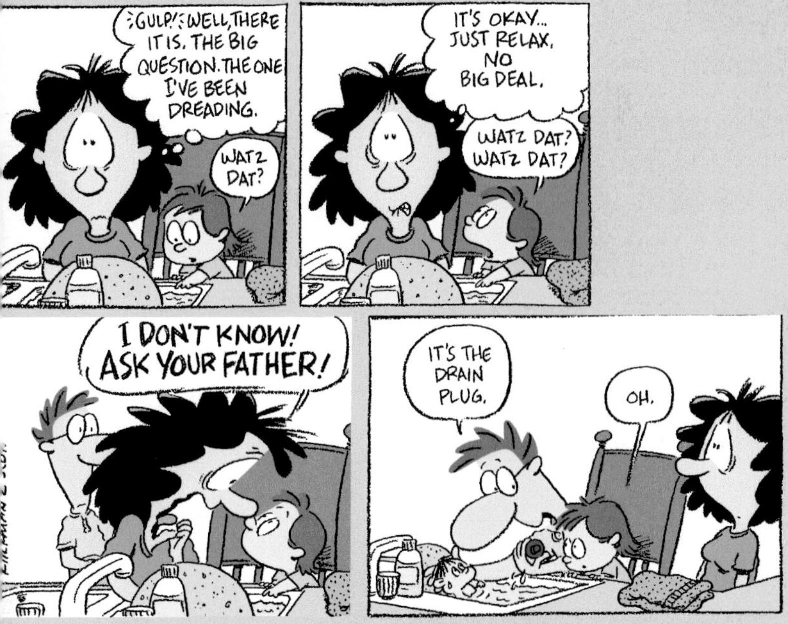
GULP! WELL, THERE IT IS. THE BIG QUESTION. THE ONE I'VE BEEN DREADING.
WATZ DAT?
IT'S OKAY... JUST RELAX. NO BIG DEAL.
WATZ DAT? WATZ DAT?
I DON'T KNOW! ASK YOUR FATHER!
IT'S THE DRAIN PLUG.
OH.

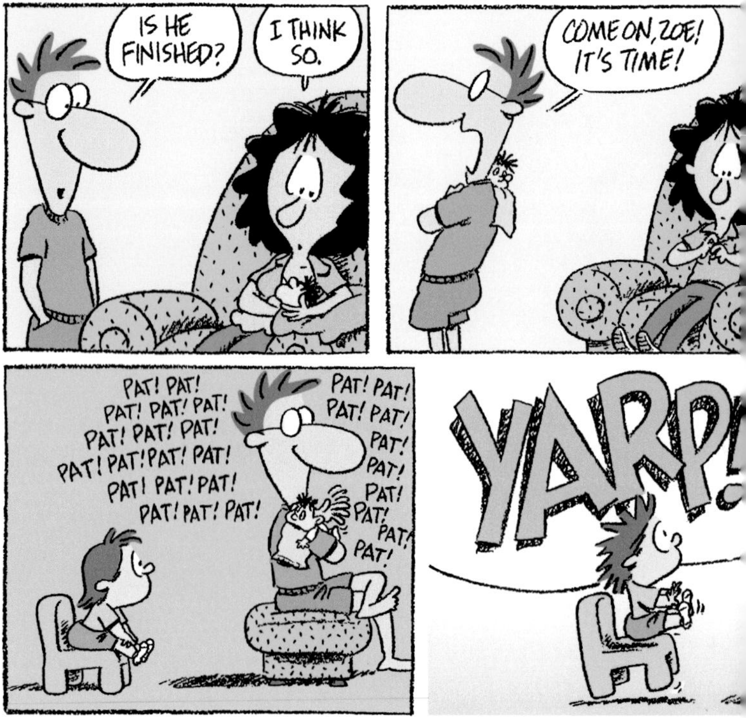
IS HE FINISHED?
I THINK SO.
COME ON, ZOE! IT'S TIME!
PAT! PAT! PAT! PAT! PAT! PAT! PAT! PAT! PAT! PAT! PAT! PAT! PAT! PAT! PAT! PAT! PAT! PAT! PAT!
PAT! PAT! PAT! PAT! PAT! PAT! PAT! PAT! PAT! PAT!
YARP!

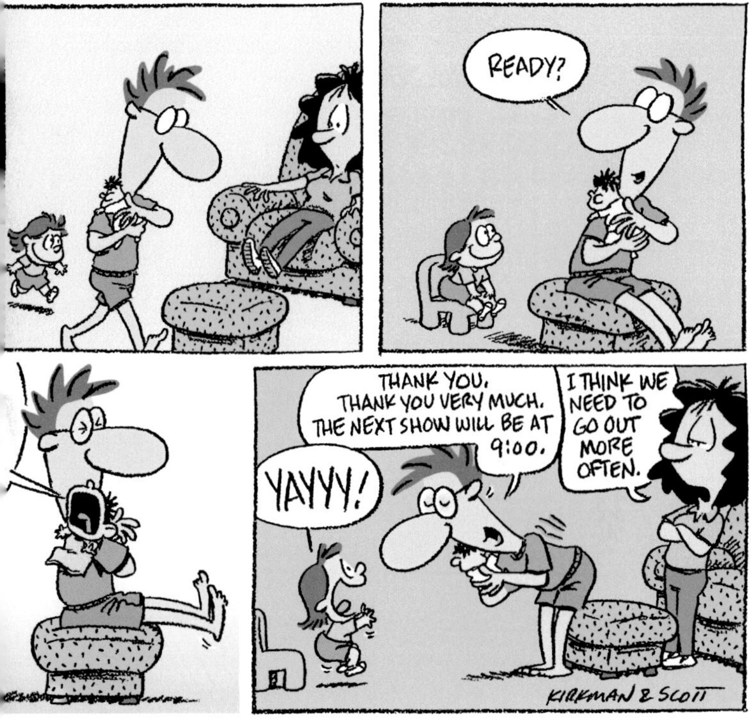
READY?
YAYYY!
THANK YOU. THANK YOU VERY MUCH. THE NEXT SHOW WILL BE AT 9:00.
I THINK WE NEED TO GO OUT MORE OFTEN.
KIRKMAN & SCOTT

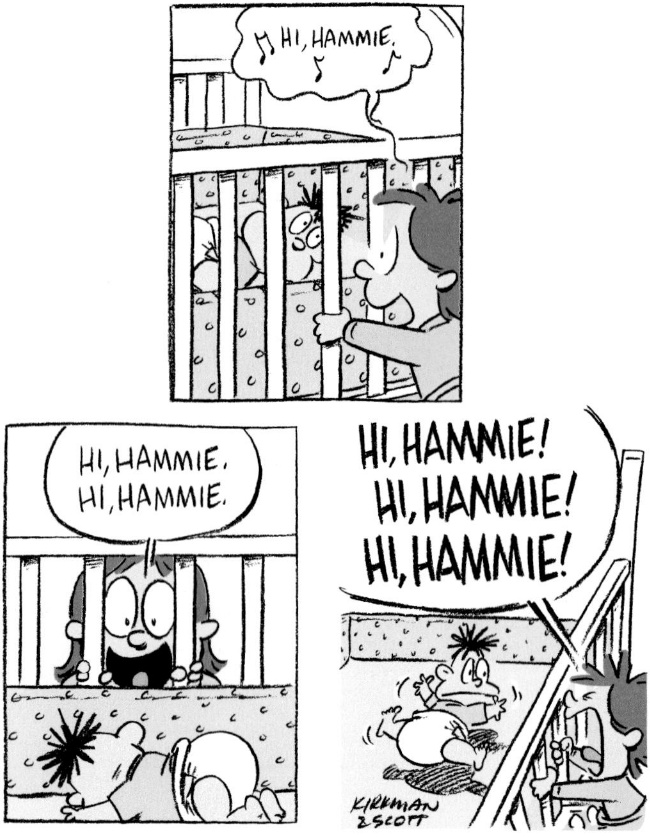
♫ HI, HAMMIE. ♪ ♪
HI, HAMMIE.
HI, HAMMIE.
HI, HAMMIE!
HI, HAMMIE!
HI, HAMMIE!
KIRKMAN & SCOTT

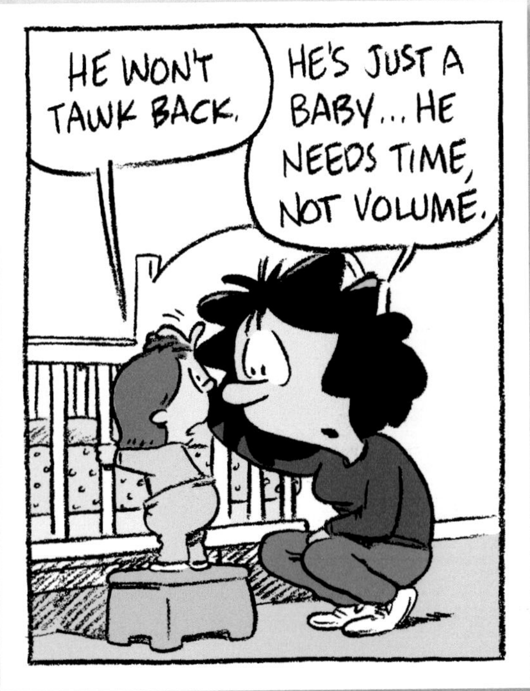
HE WON'T TAWK BACK.
HE'S JUST A BABY... HE NEEDS TIME, NOT VOLUME.

LOOK! ZOE AND HAMMIE ARE PLAYING TOGETHER!
MAYBE SHE'S FINALLY STARTING TO TREAT HIM LIKE A PERSON INSTEAD OF A TOY.
ARE YOU AND HAMMIE PLAYING HOUSE, ZOE?
YETZ. I THE MOMMY.

THAT'S NICE...
IS HAMMIE
THE BABY?
NO.
THE BROTHER?
NO.
THE DADDY?
NO.
HEEZ
THE
TABLE.
KIRKMAN & SCOTT

CHAPTER 4

NEW ROUTINE

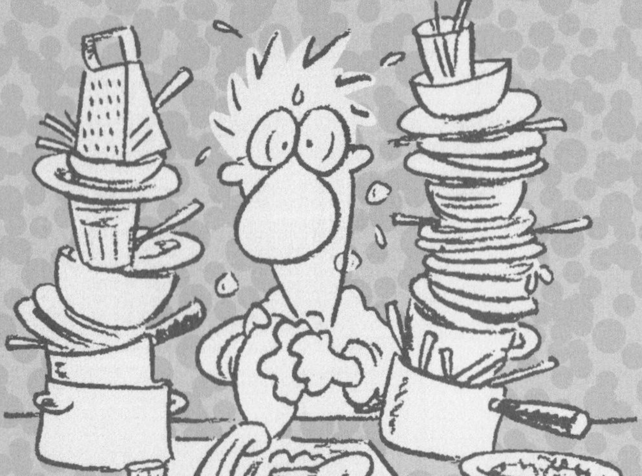

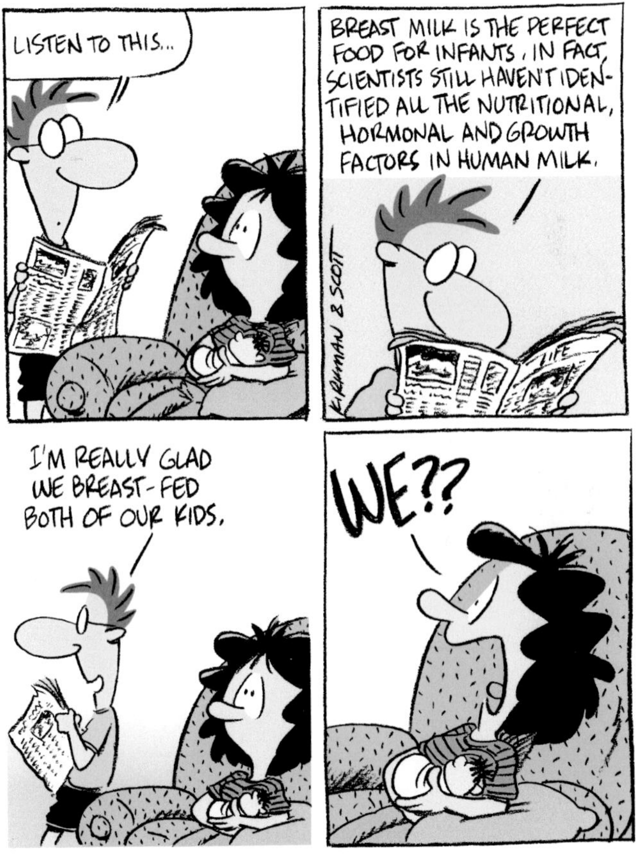
LISTEN TO THIS...
BREAST MILK IS THE PERFECT FOOD FOR INFANTS. IN FACT, SCIENTISTS STILL HAVEN'T IDENTIFIED ALL THE NUTRITIONAL, HORMONAL AND GROWTH FACTORS IN HUMAN MILK.
KIRKMAN & SCOTT
LIFE
I'M REALLY GLAD WE BREAST-FED BOTH OF OUR KIDS.
WE??

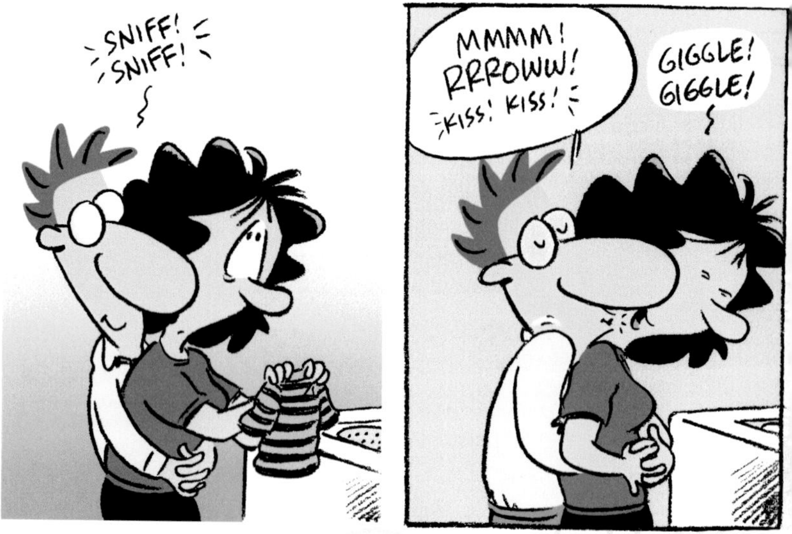
SNIFF! SNIFF!
MMMM! RRROWW! KISS! KISS!
GIGGLE! GIGGLE!

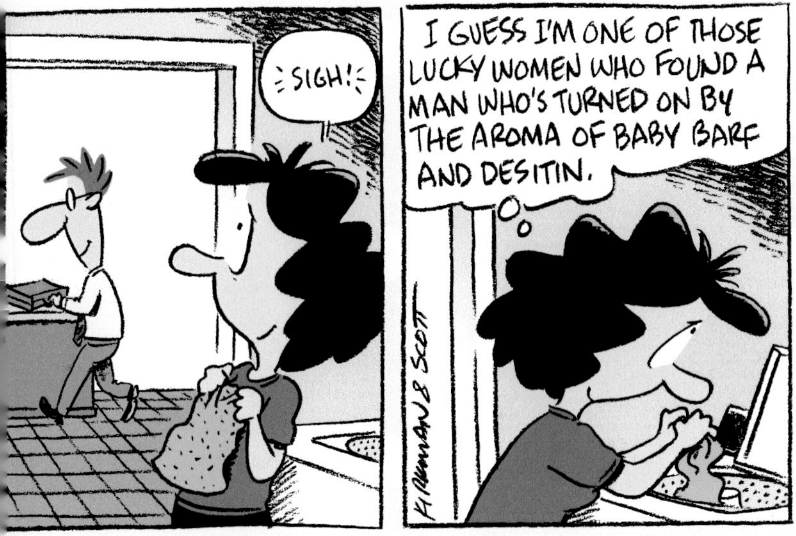
SIGH!
I GUESS I'M ONE OF THOSE LUCKY WOMEN WHO FOUND A MAN WHO'S TURNED ON BY THE AROMA OF BABY BARF AND DESITIN.
KIRKMAN & SCOTT

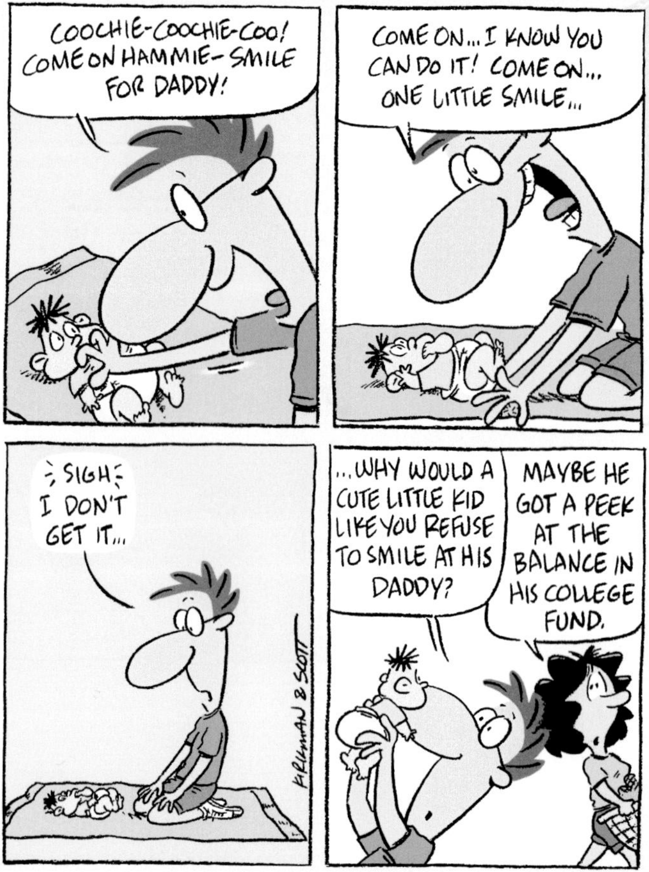
COOCHIE-COOCHIE-COO! COME ON HAMMIE- SMILE FOR DADDY!
COME ON... I KNOW YOU CAN DO IT! COME ON... ONE LITTLE SMILE...
SIGH
I DON'T GET IT...
KIRKMAN & SCOTT
...WHY WOULD A CUTE LITTLE KID LIKE YOU REFUSE TO SMILE AT HIS DADDY?
MAYBE HE GOT A PEEK AT THE BALANCE IN HIS COLLEGE FUND.

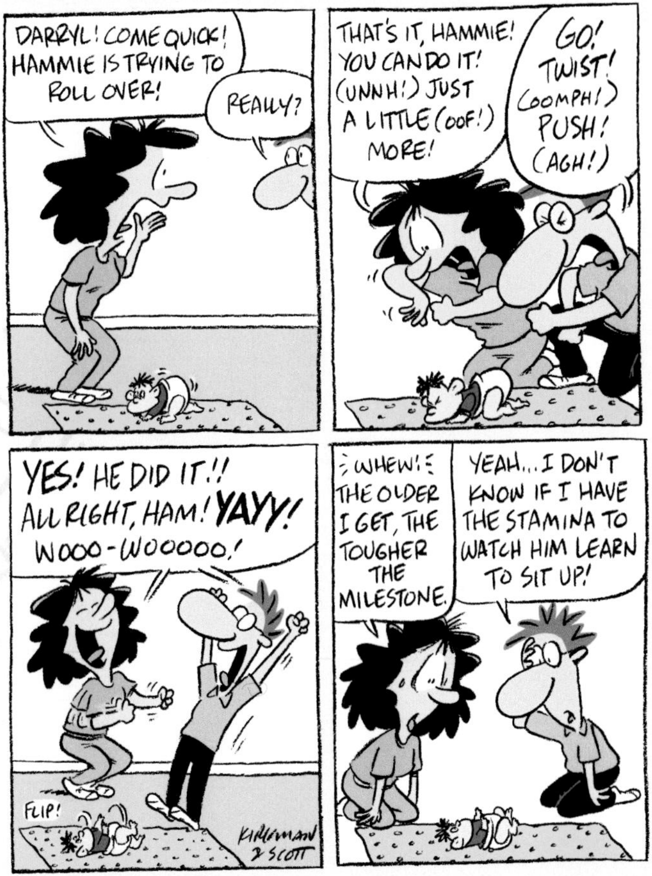
DARRYL! COME QUICK! HAMMIE IS TRYING TO ROLL OVER!
REALLY?
THAT'S IT, HAMMIE! YOU CAN DO IT! (UNNH!) JUST A LITTLE (OOF!) MORE!
GO! TWIST! (OOMPH!) PUSH! (AGH!)
YES! HE DID IT!! ALL RIGHT, HAM! YAYY! WOOO-WOOOOO!
FLIP!
KIRKMAN & SCOTT
WHEW! THE OLDER I GET, THE TOUGHER THE MILESTONE.
YEAH... I DON'T KNOW IF I HAVE THE STAMINA TO WATCH HIM LEARN TO SIT UP!

COME ON, HAMMIE! YOU CAN DO IT!
THAT'S IT! ROLL OVER! ROLL OVER!
COME ON! COME ON! JUST A LITTLE MORE!
'ATTA BOY! 'ATTA BOY! ROLL OVER!

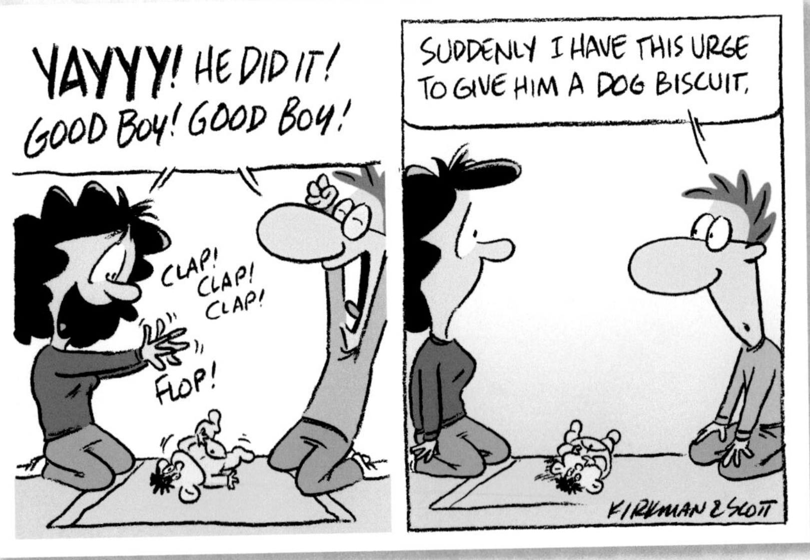
YAYYY! HE DID IT! GOOD BOY! GOOD BOY!
CLAP! CLAP! CLAP!
FLOP!
SUDDENLY I HAVE THIS URGE TO GIVE HIM A DOG BISCUIT.
KIRKMAN & SCOTT

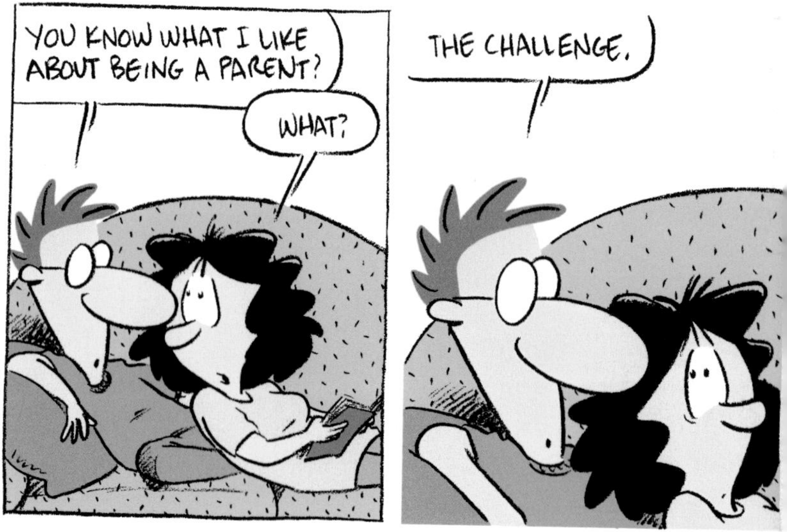
YOU KNOW WHAT I LIKE ABOUT BEING A PARENT?
WHAT?
THE CHALLENGE.

RAISING A CHILD IS MORE OF AN ART THAN A SCIENCE, AND I REALLY ENJOY THE DAY-TO-DAY INTERACTION THAT WILL SHAPE OUR KIDS INTO DECENT, RESPONSIBLE ADULTS.
WHAT'S YOUR FAVORITE THING?
THEIR BEDTIME.
KIRKMAN & SCOTT

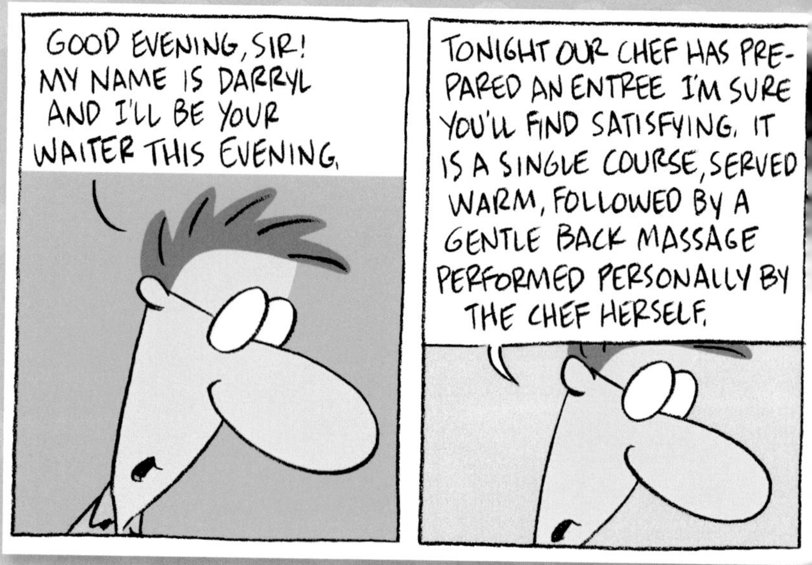
GOOD EVENING, SIR! MY NAME IS DARRYL AND I'LL BE YOUR WAITER THIS EVENING.
TONIGHT OUR CHEF HAS PREPARED AN ENTREE I'M SURE YOU'LL FIND SATISFYING. IT IS A SINGLE COURSE, SERVED WARM, FOLLOWED BY A GENTLE BACK MASSAGE PERFORMED PERSONALLY BY THE CHEF HERSELF.

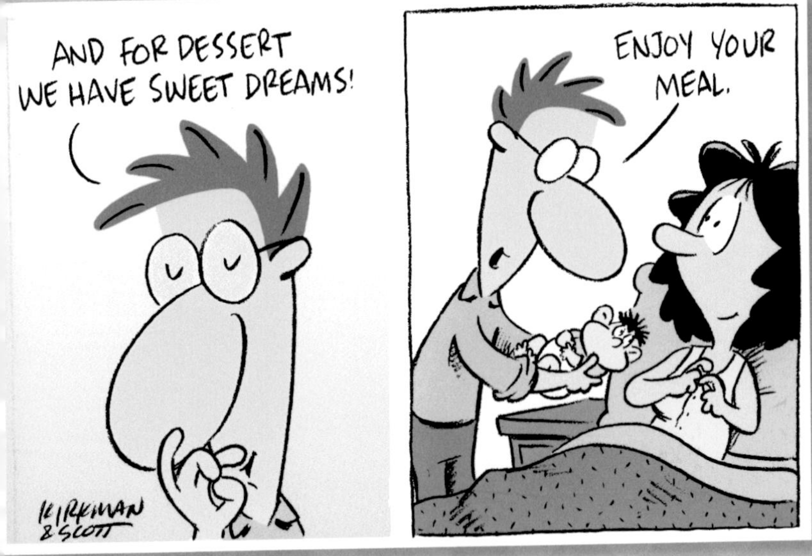
AND FOR DESSERT WE HAVE SWEET DREAMS!
ENJOY YOUR MEAL.
KIRKMAN & SCOTT

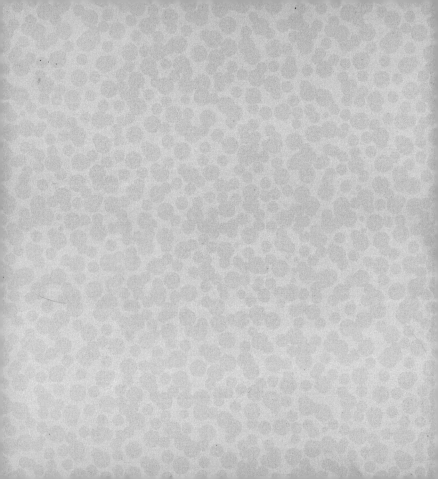